A LIFE OF
LEARNING

KARIN JOHANNISSON

A LIFE OF
LEARNING

UPPSALA UNIVERSITY
DURING FIVE CENTURIES

Editing: Uppsala University Press
Text: Karin Johannisson, Anders Lundgren
Graphic Design: Jerk-Olof Werkmäster
Translated by Max Brandt

Printed in Sweden by Bohusläningens Boktryckeri AB, 1989
© 1989 Uppsala University
ISBN 91-506-0740-5

Contents

Under the Patronage of the Church

1477–c. 1520

It was during the 15th century that Sweden began gradually to narrow the cultural lead held by the rest of Europe. At that time, general education was the domain of the cathedral schools, but all forms of higher education were still lacking. To attain the necessary academic degree entitling one to occupy an exalted position in the Church or public administration, a student of those days was obliged to travel abroad—to the Universities of Paris, Prague or Leipzig.

To remedy this regrettable state of affairs, the then Archbishop of all Sweden, Jakob Ulvsson, initiated negotiations in the 1470s for the purpose of founding a Swedish university. This was to have its seat in Uppsala, the town which by virtue of age and tradition was the country's acknowledged spiritual and secular centre. Behind this idea of a Swedish university, there lay—as elsewhere in Europe—a powerful urge to assert the virtues of the mother country. The university was intended to be not only the symbol of a burgeoning ambition for education and culture, but equally a symbol of political identity.

Following a papal sanction and pledges of legal privileges from the Privy Council, the University—the first in Scandinavia—was established in 1477. All who so wished could freely attend lectures, could defend a thesis and, after passing

CAROLINSKA ACADEMIEN

The earliest teaching at the University took place in the Chapter-House close to the Cathedral. The House was used down to the middle of the 18th century for teaching and academic disputations. From the 1620s onwards when the Gustavianum was built it was called the Old Academy or the Caroline Academy. It was demolished in 1778.

the necessary examinations, were qualified to teach. The inaugural term, in the autumn of 1477, commenced with lectures in theology, jurisprudence and philosophy.

The Privy Council, led by the Regent of Sweden, Sten Sture, had promised the University its support and stood as guarantor for the customary university privileges, the most important of which was legal autonomy: in cases involving students or university staff, the Vice-Chancellor himself would sit in judgement and pass sentence. In this way the foundations were laid for the unique position in Swedish society that the University would long enjoy.

However, there was to be no financial support from the state—the affluent Catholic Church had to shoulder that burden. The Church provided the life-blood of the University and the basis of its existence. The curriculum was designed to meet ecclesiastical needs and teaching was conducted in buildings belonging to the Cathedral. The Archbishop was the obvious choice for Chancellor and became the leading figure in the University.

THE MEDIEVAL UNIVERSITY

Little is known about the University's earliest history, and scarcely anything about its growth and organization. The first lecturers were all Swedes. There were probably six professors—all ecclesiastics. The pattern of teaching followed closely that prevailing in continental Europe. It was more a matter of reciting and commenting upon certain established texts than of proposing new ways of thinking. The pre-eminent authority—other than the theologians—was Aristotle. His all-embracing philosophy, combined with the Christian faith to form so-called

9

scholasticism, governed all scientific thinking throughout the Middle Ages. The previously accepted truths about God, the Universe and Nature became the subject of increasingly complicated academic discussion, even if they were not to be radically challenged until the scientific revolution of the 17th century.

The little we know of the University's teaching during the Middle Ages is due to a fortuitous circumstance. Among the few early students there was one, Olaus Johannis Gutho, who read at the University from 1477 to 1486. During his years of study he made assiduous notes on the professors' lectures. He collected these notes, and those of his fellow students, until eventually they filled seven tomes, which he donated to the library at Vadstena.[1] An unfortunate consequence of the Reformation was the dispersal of the treasures of Vadstena Library, though we must be thankful that Gutho's notes were eventually returned to Uppsala in the early 17th century.

These notes reveal a great deal about the onerous everyday life of students in those days. They dutifully noted down everything from their tutor's dictation, occasionally complementing the text with schematic drawings taken from the originals. Here we find transcriptions of and annotations on Aristotle's writings, illustrations of the prevailing world picture with the Earth at the centre of the universe, and comments on popular topics of controversy. Their own handwritten notes were the students' sole study material. The art of printing had only just arrived in Sweden and printed books were beyond the means of impecunious students. There was as yet no university library, though the Cathedral had its own collection, to which the professors no doubt had access.

[1] The Convent in southern Sweden founded by the Holy Birgitta, later St Birgitta.

10

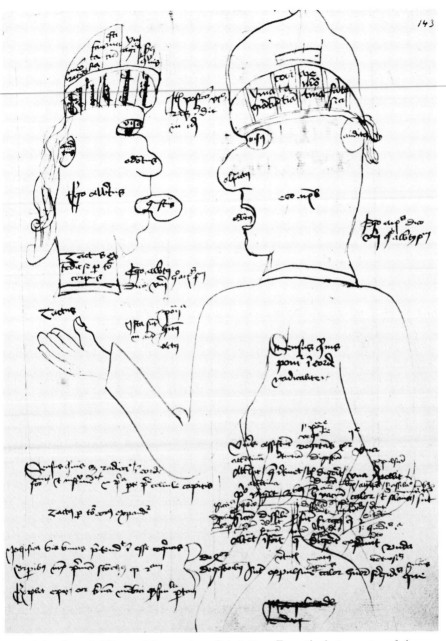

Aristotle and Albertus Magnus in a disputation. From the lecture-notes of the student, Olof Torstensson, on Aristotle's Analytica priora, *taken down in 1481.*

How did the medieval students live? We know little of their circumstances. There were in those days scarcely more than a dozen or so students at any one time. They were housed in the same fashion as cathedral scholars, in the so-called "community", a sort of lodging provided by the Church. Students probably received free board and lodging, but clothing, writing materials and all other necessities had to be brought from their homes.

The close connection between University and Church afforded a false security, a total dependence on the Archbishop's personal benevolence. Thus when Archbishop Jakob Ulvsson retired in 1515, the University stood without patronage. Teaching soon went into decline and the few lecturers and students dispersed. Sweden entered the epoch of the Reformation, a time of revolutionary crises in religion and politics, which resulted in the suppression of Catholicism in the country. And with that, the medieval university also ceased to function.

Servant of the Great Power

1593–1718

With the growth of an aggressive Protestant state under the leadership of the first Vasa kings, the prospects for Uppsala University were radically changed. The wealth of the now abolished Catholic Church had become state property and the University consequently became dependent on state support for its very existence. The Vasa kings were fully aware of the value of a university situated within the country's boundaries. The new Sweden required a spiritual hub, a stronghold for the training of state officials. At the same time the Church wanted to maintain its traditional role as bearer of culture. Attempts in the mid-16th century to get teaching on the move faltered. During the 1560s, Olof Luth lectured in Uppsala on astronomy, though this cannot be regarded as organized university education. In the 1570s, King Johan III tried to start some form of higher education at Gråmunkeholmen (Greyfriars Island) in Stockholm, but he soon fell under suspicion of trying to use this as a means to resurrect Catholicism. The attempt failed.

When Johan III died in 1592, the royal succession passed to his son, Sigismund, a Catholic, who, on his mother's side, was heir to the Polish throne. After a protracted civil war, however, Johan's brother Karl was appointed Regent and later crowned King Karl IX. Already in 1593 he had summoned the ecclesiastical and secular leaders of the land to a historical meeting in Uppsala. This assembly, known in Swedish history as The

Uppsala Meeting, was to be not only decisive for which religious persuasion the Swedish state would adopt, but it also decided that the University should be formally re-established. The state authority further granted the necessary incomes and appointed new lecturers. And so the University began to live again—this time to last.

Despite the outward serenity, however, the first years were beset by uncertainty and discord. Continental Europe was embroiled in religious wars which had everywhere developed into power politics. In Sweden, Catholicism seemed to have been crushed, Sigismund was banished and Karl IX sat securely on the throne. Yet the infant Protestant state was vulnerable and needed vigilant government, a circumstance that was also reflected in university life. These tensions were present not only in the burning religio-political controversies, but also in questions of an ideological scientific nature: mundane humanism versus traditional scholasticism, and later the rationalism of natural science versus dogmatic theology. The constellations were constantly shifting. They caused disharmony and irritation, but they also created a lively inner university life.

The accession of King Gustav II Adolf, son of Karl IX, in 1611 marked Sweden's entry into the so-called Great Power epoch. Those were the palmy days of the victorious Lutheran Church, a time of surging political expansion. In the space of a couple of decades, Sweden was transformed from a minor state into a great power. The University too was caught up in this great transformation. State support was regularized in the form of an organized development plan. It may well be that the University has never been so favoured as then, cherished by royalty, nobility and Church. The expanding state administration required capable officials, the military needed professional technicians and mathematicians, and historical research would legitimize Sweden's claims to be a great power. The Church regarded the salient position of theology at the University as a matter of prime importance. Thus the University's expansion lay in everyone's interest.

PROFESSORS AND STUDENTS

Uppsala University had been restored as Sweden's seat of learning. In a Royal Letter of 1593, the University was confirmed as a free institution for advanced studies, having special privileges in relation to society at large. No lecturer or student could be brought before a public court of criminal law, nor be taxed. Moreover, the students were entitled to free accommodation. The University was permitted to devise its own form of organization. The first statutes were enacted in 1606 on the initiative of one of the professors, Johannes Rudbeckius. Here, rules were drawn up for the University's administration and its teaching activities, for the duties of the lecturers and for student life. The duties of Vice-Chancellor, deans, bursar, cursor and proctor were all laid down—those as yet unusual titles of university officials. The University's governing body became the Senate (*konsistoriet*), in which all the professors had a seat. Minutes of Senate meetings in uninterrupted succession since 1624 have survived and constitute an invaluable historical source material.

The Royal Letter of 1593 also stated how many professors there were to be: three in theology, and one each in astronomy, physics (natural philosophy), mathematics and logic, i.e. seven altogether. During the 17th century this number was gradually increased to around 20, a figure corresponding to that applying at the larger continental universities. At first, the professors

LIBER
ACTORUM PÚ
BLICORUM CONSI.
STORII ACADEMICI
Upsaliensis.

RECTORE
Admodum Reverendo & Clariss.
viro
D. JOHANNE CAN.
LENÆO / S.S. Theol. D.
 eiusdemq; Prof. primario, & Fa-
cultatis p Senio; ac Civit. Pastore.

NOTARIO
ERICO PETI NORÆO,
Nericiensi.

himself off to the Vice-Chancellor to swear the oath of loyalty and to be enrolled in the student register. Only then could he claim the right to call himself "student".

In 1595, 70 new students were enrolled at Uppsala University, but as the years passed, the number rose until by the 1630's it had reached about 1000, where it stabilized for the rest of the 17th century. Most students were the sons of ministers of the Established Church and prior to the turn of the century the majority (65%) were educated for a religious career. Sons of the nobility comprised a surprisingly large proportion, though this included 5- to 15-year-olds. As it was *infra dig.* for a member of the nobility to place his sons in a school for the lower orders, young sons of the nobility were sent with a tutor direct to Uppsala University. Even sons of farmers were well represented—sometimes reaching about 20%, a uniquely high proportion, seen in an international perspective.

TEACHING AND UNIVERSITY LIFE

To begin with, the education offered to the students followed well-beaten tracks, best suited to future ecclesiastics and schoolteachers. It involved much theology, Aristotelian philosophy and traditional teaching in astronomy and physics (natural sciences). In Sweden, the advent of humanism, with its classical educational ideals, resulted in chairs in Greek and Hebrew. At the same time, the state powers pressed for education in political and juridical subjects. After a while, the chair in medicine,

From the Minutes of the Senate, 1641. The portrait shows King Gustav II Adolf, the Chancellor of the University Johan Skytte, Rector Magnificus Johannes Lenaeus and the Academy's Notary Ericus Noraeus.

19

long vacant, gained a new incumbent. About 1620 teaching was proceeding at all four faculties and the emphasis no longer lay on purely religious education for the ministry.

Lectures were held every day in Academia Carolina, the medieval University building situated below the Cathedral. In between times, the professors gave private so-called *kollegier* (tutorials), where in more informal small groups, students could buy extra tuition. In addition, one day per week was dedicated to oratorical exercises—in Latin. Saturday was set aside for disputations. It was in fact an amazingly ambitious educational curriculum, which was quite on a par with that offered at the major continental universities.

After about six years at the University the undergraduate was deemed ready for the decisive test: *disputation* (public defence of one's thesis). It involved writing a thesis and defending it publicly. The paper, written in Latin, was considered more as an exercise than a piece of individual research, its content as less important than irreproachable Latin and an impregnable defence. Examples of thesis titles can often seem little more than curiosities (On Angels, On the Devil, On Monsters, etc.). Nevertheless over the years these dissertations came to form a body of writing that was important as a channel for scientific information and debate. Often, it was the presiding professor who stood for the content; in the 18th century this became the rule.

The actual *disputation* came with time to follow a ritual pattern. The President (chairman presiding over the *disputation*) opened the proceedings, after which it was the occasion for appraisal and criticism from the Opponent, before finally the Respondent was given opportunity to defend his work. The entire proceeding concluded with a sumptuous feast. Outwardly, the public *disputation* still follows the same pattern as it did then; not until 1852 was the requirement abolished that the thesis be written in Latin.

The year 1600 was the first occasion in the University's history for the conferment of degrees. Fifteen students received bachelors' degrees and seven, masters' degrees. Conferment of a degree was the pinnacle of student endeavour. The Act of Conferment was built around orations in Latin and other solemn ceremonies, culminating in the award of the title *magister*, which was symbolized in a series of ceremonial acts. First there was the ascent to the lectern, signifying his newly acquired entitlement to teach. Then followed the ceremony with the book, which was first opened, and then closed. A purple hat was placed on the head of the newly created magister and a ring of gold on his ring-finger. And lastly, he received his diploma, the formal evidence of his right to instruct students.

The other great academic ceremonial function was the installation of a new Vice-Chancellor, which took place twice a year following new elections among the professors. Next to the Chancellor, the Vice-Chancellor was the University's highest authority. Starting in the early days of the 17th century, a number of new insignia were devised in keeping with his dignity. Chief of these were the twin sceptres, symbolizing his authority. Then came the seal of office, the purple cloak and the keys to the University's *carcer* (gaol) and *fiscus* (coffer). The first edition of the student membership roll was also presented and a copy of the University's Constitution. As recently as in 1877, to celebrate the University's 400th anniversary, one further item of regalia was added—the Chancellor's chain of office, in gilded silver.

The installation ceremony started early in the morning with the ringing of church-bells and a procession in strict hierarchical order through the town. The Vice-Chancellor led the way,

21

with the two cursors bearing the sceptres. This was followed in the Cathedral by a lengthy ceremony with orations and the swearing of oaths. The whole affair concluded, according to tradition, with a banquet, renowned for its sumptuousness. It was a ceremony clearly intended to impress upon the general public the privileged status enjoyed by the University.

AN EXPANDING UNIVERSITY

A never-ceasing supply of well-educated civil servants was (and still is) a precondition for any self-respecting great power. The statesmen of the day therefore pinned their faith on higher education, especially in newly conquered or distant provinces. Thus Dorpat (Tartu in Estonia) got its university as early as 1632, Turku (Finland) in 1640, Lund in 1666, while Greifswald University in Germany was restored. The universities constituted an important link in the efforts to hold together Sweden's possessions. It was no mere chance that the new university towns (apart from Lund) were also equipped at the same time with courts of appeal. But most effort was expended on Uppsala University. Even in his royal oath of 1611, Gustav Adolf had promised the University his support, no doubt with an eye to the good of the realm. In 1622 he had installed Privy Councillor, Baron Johan Skytte, as the University's Chancellor. The office of Chancellor was to function as a link between the state authorities and the University, an acknowledgement of the University as being the school for the servants of the new superpower. Those appointed Chancellor were public officials of the highest calibre—after Skytte came Axel Oxenstierna and Magnus Gabriel De la Gardie, all Privy Councillors. Thus the University was accorded the status of a royal institution with limited autonomy.

Lord Chancellor Axel Oxenstierna.

Together with Skytte and Oxenstierna, Gustav Adolf put through a series of reforms at the University. Privileges were extended and new constitutions elaborated. The number of professors was doubled and their salaries raised. All this was followed in 1624 by the munificent donation of land which gave the University a unique position as a self-sufficient institution. It meant that the University was guaranteed in perpetuity the title to large tracts of the royal estates in Uppland and Västmanland, totalling about 300 farms on Crown land. On the basis of this donation, the University would be economically solvent until the 1830s.

Of course this burgeoning of the University necessitated larger and more dignified premises than the old Carolina Academy, so the Dutchman Casper Panten was commissioned to draw up plans for new university premises immediately west of the Cathedral, to be known as the Gustavianum. This building included assembly rooms, printing-office and lecture rooms and later also the University's library and Senate Chamber.

The library too owed its creation to the King. The lack of books was still acute; the only large collection was that of the Cathedral. The new library was built up on the basis of the remnants of the medieval libraries confiscated at the time of the Reformation. Pride of place was given to the unique manuscripts from Vadstena Monastery and the Franciscan Monastery in Stockholm. The collection of books expanded with unexpected suddenness as a result of the many spoils from Swedish military campaigns on the Continent—at that time regarded as quite legitimate booty. The greatest of these treasures was the Codex Argenteus, Bishop Wulfila's Gothic transcription of the Holy Bible from the 6th century, seized by Swedish troops from the royal palace in Prague.

The library was at first housed in a small building alongside

24

ACADEMIA UPSALIENSIS GUSTAVIANA Versus Occid:

2 Theatrum Anatomicum 3 Bibliotheca Publica 4 Auditorium Majus 5 Auditorium Minus 6 Ærarium 7 Area Acad: 8 Pars Templi Cathedr. 9 Sedes Archiepiscopalis 10 Pars Consistorij Academici

The Gustavianum at the beginning of the 18th century.

the Cathedral, but was removed at the close of the 17th century to the upper floor of the Gustavianum. According to ancient library practice, not only were books kept here, but also a cabinet of curiosa and the University's collection of scientific instruments. By the turn of the century, the library had expanded to become one of the largest in northern Europe.

That the State was favourably disposed towards the University became even more evident during the reign of Queen Kristina. Spurred on by her vision of a full-blown education for future statesmen, her plan was to make the University a grand centre of culture on a European scale. Eminent German humanists were summoned as lecturers and new professorial chairs were created. Privileges were extended, chiefly as regards jurisdiction. The University's unique position vis-à-vis society at large was further accentuated.

Kristina intervened impatiently everywhere in her eagerness to create a splendid university environment. Costly literary treasures were donated to the library and the Queen's personal visits to Uppsala were the occasion for grandiose baroque events. The windlass constructed at the Castle, devised to let naked cherubs bearing bunches of grapes hover above the royal head, is just one example. Magnificence of a more enduring nature was accomplished on Kristina's orders in the new town plan, set in train in the 1640s. The old-fashioned, medieval town with its network of crooked streets and alleys was swept away, to be replaced by a chequerboard plan of regularly built residential quarters, in neoclassical fashion.

Queen Kristina was particularly solicitous for the noble students. In the new imperial state, the nobility occupied key positions, politically, economically and socially. They possessed sole right to high military and civil office. But this brought with it increasing demands for a greater degree of knowledge and training. Education specially designed for noblemen had therefore become a matter of urgency for the state. The curriculum was to be based on a secular and practical ideal: politics, modern languages, physical training (military exercises). In the 1630s, lessons were held, on paper at least, in modern languages, dancing, horsemanship and fencing, but the riding academy was not completed until the close of the century.

The question of premises for these new activities was a thorny one. The gigantic university edifice that Kristina had hoped for

Queen Kristina.

remained a dream and the new proposals put forward by Olof Rudbeck were twice rejected by the Senate (*Konsistorium*), as being far too grand. The parade ground facilities—in their ultimate form according to revised plans by Rudbeck—were a concession to the economic realities of the time—a simple single storey building with two wings embracing a gravel yard.

After all this restoration work, the University had been virtually rebuilt from its foundations. As regards the question of professors and numbers of students, it compared favourably with the more eminent continental universities. In return, the state powers required that the University serve the realm. Provision of the hall for *exercitier* (fencing, riding, dancing, music, etc.) and the parade ground was a move in this direction. The education of state servants was expanded, with studies in juridical and humanistic subjects. But how did other subjects fare?

THEOLOGY AND THE NEW WORLD PICTURE

No other faculty during Sweden's Great Power era had greater prestige than theology. The Church occupied an undisputed position as comrade-in-arms of the secular state power— Lutheran orthodoxy was regarded as a precondition for national unity. The objective of theology in the 17th century was therefore to establish for the good of the Church and of the state, the true faith and to defend it from all heresies which might endanger society. The Aristotelian world view was also exploited by the Church in this effort. Every attempt to escape from the accepted world of ideas was immediately combatted: the Copernican world picture, which claimed that the sun—and not the earth—was the centre of the universe, came to symbolize the challenge to existing thought.

But from the mid-17th century, new ideas began to filter into the traditional university world of thought. The new natural sciences claimed that Nature herself—and not ancient authorities—would provide the scientists with solutions to their problems. Faced with this radical new view, the medieval concept could not prevail and Aristotelian science collapsed. The conflict was most acutely felt in the so-called Cartesian battles (named after one of the foremost champions of the new view of Nature, the Frenchman Descartes), during the latter half of the 17th century. What the dispute primarily turned on was the pre-eminence of the theological faculty at the University versus the demand from other faculties to be allowed to conduct free scientific investigation. In this struggle, the Cartesian world picture was used as a handy weapon. When hostilities ceased, about 1690, the new science emerged, it is true, as victor, but with strict orders not to discuss the basic theological dogmas.

OLOF RUDBECK

In the foreground of the new age stood Olof Rudbeck, universal genius. His versatility was astounding. He made his own independent contributions in the fields of anatomy, botany, mechanics, music and archaeology. He even showed considerable talent as an intriguer and university politician. In the Cartesian controversy he took a clear stand on the side of the new science. In inspired building projects, both the practical ones and the products of his fantasy, he embodied Sweden's dreams of national and international prowess.

As early as 1650, the 19-year-old medical student Rudbeck had made what has been called Sweden's first independent contribution in natural science. By undertaking methodical

Olof Rudbeck.

dissection of about 400 animal, Rudbeck succeeded in charting the course and function of the lymphatic vessels. The news spread quickly and Rudbeck was summoned to Uppsala Castle to demonstrate his discovery before Queen Kristina, and in 1653 it was made known to the world at large. Rudbeck's discovery lent support to the current revolution in physiology which had been initiated with William Harvey's discovery of blood circulation, and helped destroy, at last, the ancient dogmas that had dominated medicine through the Middle Ages.

As Professor of Medicine from 1660, Rudbeck together with his colleague, Petrus Hoffvenius, made a great effort to improve teaching. No subject was so divorced from applied research as medicine. The gap between the practical art of healing and medicine at the University was great. Often there were no more than two or three students present each term. The Chancellor intervened time and again, stipulated that an anatomical demonstration should be held publicly once a year, and apportioned funds for the purchase of instruments. But no demonstrations took place.

It was no easy task in those days to obtain human corpses for anatomical demonstrations and the antipathy towards those who cut up dead bodies was considerable—"people call the anatomist 'executioner'". It was a miracle that Rudbeck could make any headway under such conditions. But he, more than any other, realised the importance of teaching in anatomy. However, there was nowhere suitable for anatomical demonstrations to take place in—so Rudbeck built his own premises. In 1662–63 he constructed on the roof of Gustavianum, a Theatrum anatomicum, a circular temple-like hall with a cupola roof, and room for 200 observers on tiered benches arrayed around the dissection slab. The similarity to a religious temple was altogether intentional—anatomical dissections were not

31

merely medical demonstrations, but intended ultimately to reveal how perfect God's creation was, how wonderfully and miraculously the human body was designed.

In practice, the anatomical theatre was used only on a few occasions. The difficulty of obtaining corpses was still an obstacle—only the bodies of criminals, suicides and illegitimate children were permitted anatomical subjects. But Rudbeck made sure that the few dissections that did take place were turned into theatrical spectacles. In a printed programme, he invited the general public (for a pecuniary consideration) to witness the performance. By way of introduction, eulogistic poems to the deceased were read, and after the dissection was concluded, those present were invited to follow the corpse to the graveside.

Rudbeck's medical professorship also included botany, a traditional part of medical skills. In the late 1650s he laid out in the Svartbäck district of Uppsala a botanical garden (nowadays known as the Linnéan Gardens), which he filled with both indigenous and exotic plants, not only for the students to wander among and study, but also to supply the pharmacists with useful medicinal plants and herbs.

But Rudbeck did not rest content with the stock of plants provided by his botanical garden. With his inexhaustible energy he took upon himself the gargantuan task of producing a collection of engraved prints, based on woodcuts, illustrating plants from all over the world. The inspiration for this was the superb so-called Burser herbarium which came into the University's possession in the form of war booty; in addition there were plants that Rudbeck himself had collected and gifts from foreign botanists. The whole project was an enormous undertaking. Finance was arranged from private patrons, a staff of woodcarvers were employed, including several of Rudbeck's own children, and work commenced. Every plant was sketched in natural size and then carved in wood. At the same time, a series of hand-painted plates was produced. After only a few years, they had completed 1,200 printing blocks and the whole work is estimated to comprise over 10,000 prints. 1701 saw the completion of the first volume of *Campus Elysii*—the Elysian Fields—and in 1702 came volume two. It was at this juncture that the Great Fire devastated Uppsala. This was a catastrophe not only for the whole town, but also for Rudbeck, who saw his life's work consumed by the flames. Seven thousand blocks and almost the entire printed edition burned up in the space of a few hours. Today only a few wooden blocks remain and of *Campus Elysii's* first edition, just two priceless examples. "I and my wife are as rich now as when we lay in the crib, all my works... all burned. The Lord giveth and the Lord taketh away, blessed be His name eternally." So commented Rudbeck in his hour of despair.

Yet the subject that came to be Rudbeck's particular interest above all others was neither medicine nor botany. Towards the close of his life he devoted all his energy to something regarded then as lying far beyond the realm of scientific reality: Gothic archaeology.

With a long tradition behind it, Gothic historical romance experienced a powerful renaissance during the reign of Gustav II Adolf. It was a view of history characterized by romantic patriotism. In different ways, it was felt desirable to show that Sweden, the land of the Goths, had in byegone days been the cradle of the whole of western civilization. At first a mere daydream, the idea became during Gustav's reign a natural expression of a profound feeling of national self-esteem and at the same time a moral justification for the expansive foreign policy then obtaining. Archaeology received every encouragement—a special department of the Civil Service was set up to

33

The Tree of Japhet. From Olof Rudbeck's Atalantica. *Rudbeck claimed that the Swedes were descended from Noah's son, Japhet, and were the ancestors of all other peoples. To the left of the Tree of Christianity can be seen the Tree of Japhet planted in Sweden. The apples that have fallen down symbolize the different peoples of the world.*

deal with the gathering of "antiquities" and a professor in the history of the fatherland was appointed.

The acme of this Gothic tradition is represented by Rudbeck's mammoth work *Atland*, or *Atlantica* (1679–1702), the most celebrated book to be produced in Uppsala during the 17th century. Using a massive collection of data, Rudbeck elaborated on the myth of a territory in the far north called the Land of the Hyperboreans, reputed to be a paradise of prosperity and culture, which had let its superabundance flow out to a needy world. To this theme, Rudbeck added the myth of Atlantis, the tales of the drowned islands related by Plato. Rudbeck was in no doubt–Atlantis and Sweden were one and the same. With the keen eye of a sleuth, he combed classical literature, gleaning items of information that could support his case. In place-names, maps, ancient monuments, myths and tales, he sought his comparative material. The ancient Egyptian Thebes was actually Täby (a place just north of Stockholm) (!), Troy was Trögd (in the diocese of Uppsala), etc. He unearthed new evidence everywhere; in this way Sweden was transformed into the birthplace and source of all cultures. Yet his methods, even in archaeology, were at the same time those of modern natural science. For instance, he dated graves in true experimental manner: first he measured the accretion of humus during one year within an experimental plot and then by comparing the depth of soil above the grave, he could establish its age. In this way, historical speculation and modern natural scientific methods were combined in Rudbeck's work to form a synthesis.

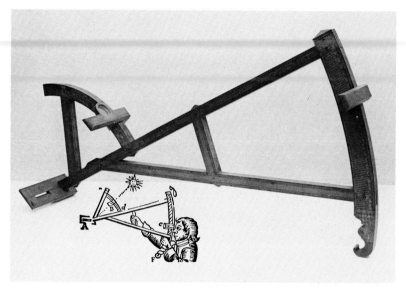

Quadrant, the second half of the 17th century. From the University Collection of Astronomical Instruments.

MATHEMATICS, ASTRONOMY AND NATURAL HISTORY

In society as it emerged during the Great Power epoch, access to scientific and technical expertise was a necessity. During the 17th century, mathematics became a key science, an indispensable art. University mathematics included, in addition to astronomy, geometry and algebra, mechanics, chronology and a knowledge of instruments, also theories on globes, charts and sundials. Starting around the mid-17th century, applied mathematics found increasing use in everyday life. The military sphere, land surveying, mining—all were seen to be dependent on reliable technical expertise; the training of engineers and land surveyors was a new challenge for the University.

Within all this patriotic scientific research, there was an

36

aspiration among Swedes to increase the fund of historical and cultural knowledge of their own country. Not least was it a matter of being aware of all that was particularly and typically Swedish. In 1671 the Uppsala professor, Johannes Schefferus, was made responsible by the authorities for preparing a printed description of Lapland, with the realization in mind that everything to do with arctic Scandinavia was exotic material, much sought after abroad. Schefferus carried out his commission in a couple of years—without having so much as set foot in Lapland! He obtained his material from older sources and reports sent in by clergymen in Lapland. *Lapponia* (1673) was a broad account of the scenery and inhabitants of those parts, illustrated with woodcuts made from Schefferus' own sketches. As hoped, the book became an international success—the magical aura surrounding everything Nordic was irresistible.

The exploration of Lapland was continued along completely different lines by the younger Olof Rudbeck, the eminent father's son and successor to the Chair of Medicine. Accompanied by two wood-carvers, Rudbeck travelled north during the 1690's; this time it was a question of working scientifically, and of being on the spot to portray and document Lapland's flora and fauna. Rudbeck planned to publish his findings in a large-scale work, *Lapponia illustrata*. However, his life's work too was devastated by the Great Fire mentioned earlier. Only the preface to this book appeared and only remnants of his mammoth material collection have survived to this day.

As a botanist, Rudbeck was distinguished, but as a zoologist he was a true pioneer. Zoology in the 17th century was meagre and riddled with myths and exotic ideas. The literature of university dissertations seldom strayed beyond the world of fables. But Rudbeck broke with the tradition that held that creatures in literature were more interesting than real-life ani-

1   2

3   4

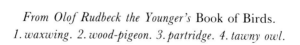

From Olof Rudbeck the Younger's Book of Birds.
1. waxwing. 2. wood-pigeon. 3. partridge. 4. tawny owl.

mals. His great book of birds, including over 200 hand-painted plates, marks the advent of scientific zoology to Sweden. It was intended to be a general inventory of Swedish birds, but was made use of in Rudbeck's lectures, as a teaching aid. Since stuffed exhibits did not exist at that time, Rudbeck held up his illustrations, pointed and explained. For the students, starved of concrete material, Rudbeck's illustrations were a revelation: "they appeared not to be the work of Man" (Linné).

MEDICINE

Despite all the efforts of Rudbeck the Elder, instruction in medicine continued to be inadequate throughout the 17th century. In order to achieve the doctor's degree necessary to become a practising physician, the students of those days had to travel abroad. But even basic training in Uppsala was neglected. The younger Rudbeck had little interest in medicine and it was left to Lars Roberg, professor from 1697 to 1740, to bear the brunt of the teaching chores.

Roberg was innovative and independent. Among other things, he introduced new teaching aids such as illustrations and sketches that were passed around among the students. He also wrote the first textbook on anatomy in Swedish, *Lijkrevningstavlor* (1718). At the Latin-dominated University this was something quite novel—a textbook in one's native tongue; what was more, the language was shockingly, even outspokenly frank and many of the anatomical details had been given Roberg's own personal appellations. Some passages were too strong for the Censor's department to stomach; Roberg was obliged to replace them with revised text.

Roberg realised the need for the students to have a practical

Lars Roberg, drawing of a foetus, beginning of the 18th century.

medical training. But dissections took place only sporadically and opportunity to demonstrate directly at the bedside was non-existent. The older Rudbeck had tried in the 1660s to set up a university hospital in Uppsala, but it fell to Roberg to implement these plans. It was the financial question that proved the most difficult obstacle. The University felt disinclined to contribute. But Roberg was importunate, succeeded in getting the Collegium Medicum in Stockholm to provide the basic funding, begged some of the money and contributed the rest himself. In 1708 the so-called Oxenstiernska House at Riddartorget in Uppsala was bought as premises for the academic hospital (Nosocomium academicum). That funds were scanty, to say the least, is evidenced by Roberg's modest proposals for running expenses: he asks for funds to purchase *one* bed with bed linen, food for *one* patient, plus medicaments and dressings.

The hospital never fulfilled Roberg's hopes. Admittedly he carried on both clinical and polyclinical treatment. A few operations were also carried out, usually in public, for the purpose of improving the hospital's meagre economy by charging admission fees. But it was these financial obstacles that were and continued to be insuperable. Without assistance from the University, Roberg was left to manage matters as best he could by renting out parts of the premises. Patients were few, sometimes none at all and teaching occasionally had to be abandoned altogether. The building gradually became delapidated and all activities ceased completely during the 1720s.

In the Service of Utilitarianism

1720–c. 1800

The year 1718 ushered in a new political era in Sweden. The wounds from the years of war still smarted; no one could avoid noticing that. Sweden had been drained of manpower and capital, been reduced from a great power to an insignificant minor state on the edge of Europe. The situation called for quick remedies. In the economic field, mercantilism was making a vigorous breakthrough with a call for a development plan based on a stocktaking and a processing of native resources.

Simultaneously with the upheavals in foreign affairs, the autocratic monarchy collapsed, to be replaced by an elected parliament as the dominant power in domestic matters. The first political parties made their entrance—two to start with, named after their preferred headgear, the "Hats" and the "Caps". The Hats found their supporters among the nobility active in public affairs. They regarded the existence of a full-blown state apparatus as a necessity of life. They propagandized energetically in the cause of mercantilism combined with a utilitarian outlook on life. The country's indigenous natural resources must be explored and charted; trade and manufacture, agriculture and mining encouraged and developed. When the Hats came to power in 1738, public utilitarianism became the fashionable catchword. The manufacturing industry was founded, agricultural reforms carried out and Sweden's rulers hoped to consolidate the economy around domestic production of commodities and increased export of iron.

The University was divided in its response to the new ideology. Academic freedom was sometimes felt to be endangered by the strict control applied by the state authorities. On the other hand, the education and training of new generations of state officials was just as much of national concern now as during the earlier, imperial era. It was necessary to train officials who believed in and had a grasp of the new economic ideology and who would be able to put it to work for the good of the country. The University succeeded, not without great effort, in averting a proposed reform that would have abolished the old faculty system, discontinued "unnecessary" disciplines and directed resources to the building up of new blocks of subjects directly oriented to certain professions and trades.

But at the same time the new economic policy was profoundly stimulating, especially for the natural sciences. In the name of utilitarianism, researchers received strong, almost passionate support. The atrophying academic departments were infused with new life and purpose, new departments were set up and disciplines such as economics, chemistry and physics each received a chair. Led by such outstanding scientists as Linnaeus, Celsius, Klingenstierna, Torbern Bergman, and others, an open-minded and revitalised scientific research made rapid advances and soon transformed Uppsala University into a world-renowned seat of learning. Now started a period of unsurpassed greatness, when foreign students flocked to Uppsala and scientific work was conducted with unprecedented enthusiasm.

NATIONAL ECONOMY — ANDERS BERCH

Highly characteristic of the period was the parliamentary decision of 1739 to create a professorship in political economics, in

The Theatrum oeconomico-mechanicum in the Old Square.

other words, economy with the emphasis on agriculture, mining and manufacturing. The decision was taken without consulting the University and without granting the necessary financial resources. By virtue of its interdisciplinary nature, the subject constituted a guarantee for the spread of utilitarianism throughout the University. Parliament also assumed the right to appoint their man to the post and their choice fell on Anders Berch, a clerk from Stockholm without any real academic qualifications. In this way Parliament demonstrated its power by setting aside in the name of the public interest the customary University procedures.

Berch took up the Chair in 1741. His teaching comprised economic and legal subjects as well as natural history and mechanics. Appointed by Parliament but financially dependent on the University, Berch found himself in a difficult situation. The State made it quite plain that he was their man—his teaching was kept under constant observation and a journal of his lectures was required to be kept as a check.

Berch's first task was to acquire premises for the department. In the absence of state funds and faced with disinterest on the part of the University, Berch was forced to appeal to wealthy businessmen for financial help with the project. By 1754 he was in a position to purchase an old property facing Gamla Torget (the Old Square). Here, the so-called Theatrum oeconomico-mechanicum was developed into a thriving Department with many students. Ironically, the University soon regarded it as one of its own and proudly proclaimed it "one of the stateliest establishments of the entire Academy"!

In the large lecture-hall, Berch held lectures in the conventional manner, but also practical demonstrations by means of unique teaching aids. These were models in miniature depicting agricultural tools and machines, samples of raw materials, animal, vegetable and mineral, materials in various stages of pro-cessing, as well as examples of finished products. This demon-stration material is extraordinarily interesting from a pedagogic point of view. The idea was that the student should not only learn how to carry out financial calculations, but also be able to put that knowledge into practice. What tools were used in agriculture, in mining? How could production be increased? Productivity? What were the various stages in the processing of an article, from raw material to finished product? In possession of such knowledge, Uppsala graduates were now well equipped to step into responsible positions in commerce and industry—a science more "applied" than could ever have been imagined.

ASTRONOMY—ANDERS CELSIUS

That the University defended itself from too rigid a state control did not blind it to the advantages of utilitarianism. When Anders Celsius—already an internationally known astro-nomer—applied in 1738 for funds with which to found an astronomical observatory in Uppsala, he made use of a prop-aganda pamphlet in which he adroitly drew attention to the advantages to society of such an observatory. Here, instructors in navigation could be trained, meteorological log-books be kept and data be collected for the production of maps.

The Senate immediately granted 17,000 riksdaler toward the purchase and conversion of the so-called "Billbergska" house on Svartbäck Street (now known as Celsius House) and during the following years, a further 16,000 towards procuring the necessary instruments. Celsius had thus succeeded in obtaining altogether 33,000 riksdaler, an unheard sum of money in those days. No other professor was blessed with such financial resources for many a long day.

Anders Celsius.

Celsius had taken up his duties as professor in 1730, but following academic tradition he spent his first year in making a detailed tour of the continent. He had caused a sensation everywhere with his astronomical observations. In Rome the Pope placed an observatory at his disposal and while in Paris he was invited to participate, together with the famous Maupertuis, in an expedition to Lapland for the purpose of settling the question of the shape of the Earth at the Poles, by measuring the length of a degree along the meridian. The Expedition of 1736–37 attracted attention throughout Europe and Celsius returned home a hero. At the Uppsala Observatory he continued with his astronomical observations concerning the nature of the aurora borealis, the light intensity of the stars, and the formation of constellations. He made more than 6,000 measurements in investigations into the influence of terrestrial magnetism on the magnetized needle.

The invention of the hundred-degree thermometer scale, with the boiling point and freezing point of water as the two fixed points, has made the name Celsius known throughout the world. At that time it was generally believed impossible for the same fixed points to apply under differing geographical and meteorological conditions. By his careful experimental work, however, Celsius showed that snow always melts at the same point on the scale, whether it be in Lapland or in Skåne, out in the open or in a bowl before an open fire. In 1742 he presented his thermometer before the Academy of Sciences. There he fixed 100° as the freezing point for water and 0° as its boiling point. It was not until after his death that the scale was reversed to give the scale used today.

At the time the observatory came into use in 1741 it was considered to be very well equipped. However, it soon became apparent that the location of the building was far from ideal.

Smoke from houses in the neighbourhood impaired visibility and busy street traffic rendered precise measurement difficult. Nevertheless the old observatory served its purpose until 1853, when a new one was built on Rackarberget (Gallows hill) on the northwestern outskirts of Uppsala.

PHYSICS — SAMUEL KLINGENSTIERNA

Physics too was one of the favoured disciplines that received considerable support in the spirit of the times. The subject had long been part of medical teaching and it was only now that it emerged as an independent subject. The vicissitudes surrounding the creation of the chair in physics—like that in chemistry—reflect clearly the arguments heard in the current debate. The uses to which physics could be applied in industry were obvious and Parliament called for training at university level. The crucial question was, however, how these professorships should be financed (one must bear in mind that the University was intended to be self-supporting). One after another the solutions were discussed, and it was not until 1750 that an acceptable compromise was devised: if two "unnecessary" subjects, poetry and oriental languages, were abolished the funds so released could be transferred to the two new chairs. And this is what happened for a while and the hastily appointed professors could take up their posts that very same year.

The obvious choice for the chair in physics was Samuel Klingenstierna, Professor of Mathematics for the past 20 years. Like Celsius, Klingenstierna had spent part of his professorial career in study travels abroad, where he had made useful contacts with leading European natural scientists and at the same time received a thorough schooling in mathematics and

49

Microscope of the Culpeper-type. From the Samuel Klingenstierna Collection of Instruments, purchased 1739.

physics. On his return home, he commenced demonstrations in experimental physics, which soon achieved enormous popularity. The hitherto somnolent lecture sessions were transformed into stimulating theatrical performances, where the students could witness the wondrous powers of Nature at play.

These public experimental displays had commenced under the auspices of the (British) Royal Society, but were soon introduced into university education, not to mention their use in the workshops of the more prestigious instrument-makers in London. The favourites were a variety of optical phenomena and demonstrations of air-pumps, electricity machines and the Leyden jar, but spectators could also reverentially observe the world through the microscope and telescope.

Klingenstierna's collection of instruments is a representative example of the equipment of an 18th century physicist. The collection is nowadays unique of its kind. The instruments were purchased in England during the years 1739–43 for a total sum of 5,470 riksdaler. Here we find the magic lantern, an early type of projector which cast images onto a screen, with nothing more than a wax candle as light source. The pictures, hand-painted glass plates, were supplied together with the lantern. Especially popular subjects were biblical characters, or devils and trolls, with which to titillate the imagination of the spectator sitting in the dark. Another showpiece was the air pump which demonstrated what happened when air was evacuated from, or compressed in a sealed glass globe. As demonstration material small animals or birds were often placed in the globe, thus treating the spectator to a gruesome spectacle. Electrical apparatuses and the Leyden jar also lent themselves to impressive demonstrations. The Leyden jar in particular was an excellent and easily handled object with which to impress spectators with the wonderful properties of electricity. Vast quantities of electricity

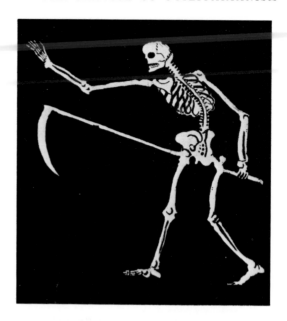

Picture-slides for the magic lantern. From the Samuel Klingenstierna Collection of Instruments, purchased in 1739.

could be stored in the jar, later to be released at will. Klingenstierna also amused himself with the Leyden jar in more private experiments: "many a time we despatched the electrified jar to friends round about town, who got a tremendous shock from it"!

Klingenstierna's name is especially associated with the development of the telescope. It had been introduced early in the 17th century and had been successively improved, though even in the mid-18th century one of its main drawbacks was still unsolved: the scattering of light (chromatic aberration), which arose during the refraction of light through the lens and which blurred the image. Newton had asserted that the problem was insoluble and, by virtue of his authority, inhibited further attempts at a solution. However, Klingenstierna questioned Newton's conclusions and was able by geometrical means to demonstrate his thesis. He sent his evidence to England's leading instrument-maker, John Dollond, who soon succeeded in constructing a double lens which neutralized the colour refraction. The new objective allowed study of celestial bodies to be made with a new degree of sharpness, and played an important part in the advance of astronomy during the 18th century.

CHEMISTRY—JOHAN GOTTSCHALK WALLERIUS AND TORBERN BERGMAN

The University's first Professor of Chemistry was appointed in 1750, at the expense of the subject Poetry which, according to the Hat Party's way of thinking was nothing more than a "decorative amusement". Chemistry, on the other hand, would be of use in a variety of ways in agriculture, mining and the production of pharmaceuticals.

Even during the 17th century chemistry had been an important science in Sweden, mainly by virtue of its obvious uses in the economically important mining industry. Its centre up to 1750 was the Laboratorium Chymicum at the Mining College (*Bergskollegium*) in Stockholm. Chemistry as a university discipline had formed part of Medicine, and had been primarily directed to what was called *materia medica*, i.e. the production of medicaments and drugs.

When Johan Gottschalk Wallerius was appointed first incumbent of the professorial chair, the department was still without premises—all teaching in chemistry had hitherto been carried on at the medical faculty. The Senate took the decision to go to the expense of providing chemistry with its own new-built premises. In 1754, Laboratorium Chemicum stood ready for use, with its two laboratories—one larger, for lectures, and a smaller one for individual work with students.

Even though Wallerius carried out useful pioneering work in agricultural chemistry, activities at the new laboratories were soon dominated by mineral analyses and the arranging of collections of minerals. For the purchase and maintenance of instruments, Wallerius received an annual appropriation of 200 riksdaler plus a ration of two loads of charcoal from the University's forests. In order to improve the Department's meagre economy, Wallerius started production of chemical-based medicaments which were sold to the apothecaries. Both Wallerius and his successor, Torbern Bergman, bear witness to the fact that a chemist's life then was a hard one—both became ill from their long daily stint in the unhealthy laboratories, sometimes in the heat of the furnace, always on the icy cold stone floor and chilled by draughts. Bergman says "At every lecture I was so frozen that when I had gone to bed I could not get warm and go to sleep before four in the morning".

Torbern Bergman.

When Bergman took office in 1767 after Wallerius, Swedish 18th century chemistry entered a new period of greatness. At the same time, at the University Pharmacy on the other side of the River Fyris, Scheele was carrying on his pioneering experiments. When Bergman became professor, he had already studied entomology, astronomy and physics, though more for his own enlightenment than because he was especially gifted in those subjects.

The Laboratorium Chemicum had already begun to fall into disrepair. The wretched circumstances under which Wallerius had to work are evidenced by the scanty collection of instruments at his disposal: just a few mortars and crucibles. Bergman, however, obtained funds with which to re-equip the laboratories and within a few years he had succeeded in raising standards to a high level.

Bergman had great ability both as teacher and as a researcher. His work was encouraged and supported financially by Gustav III and by the Academy of Sciences. His reputation was also enhanced by the numerous foreign disciples he attracted to the Department. He was a brilliant analyst and devised several new analytical methods. Among his other achievements are elucidation of the properties of carbon dioxide, tables of chemical affinity (tables showing the propensity of chemical substances to react with one another), and a new chemical nomenclature. It was Bergman who kept alive the traditions of research in Uppsala during the Age of Liberty down to the 1780s.

MEDICINE—NILS ROSÉN VON ROSENSTEIN

By the time of what is known in Sweden as the "Age of Liberty", teaching in medicine at Uppsala had virtually ceased.

Nils Rosén von Rosenstein.

The University hospital that Lars Roberg had managed to start had never functioned satisfactorily. The building was now dilapidated and had been let out as a tavern and also served as the haunt of itinerant theatre companies. There was no clinical instruction and no dissections were undertaken. Indeed the faculty actually had no more than a handful of students. The medical profession was scarcely one that attracted; there was widespread mistrust of an occupation that had little more to offer its clients than medieval palliatives and remedies.

But all this was transformed with the rise of the mercantile ideology, according to which the source of any nation's greatness was a large population and to achieve this goal it was necessary to invest in an extended medical service. The first hospitals were therefore founded and the numbers of district physicians increased. When in 1740 Carl von Linné (Linnaeus) and Nils Rosén (von Rosenstein) were appointed professors of medicine, optimism rose.

The University hospital was renovated and opened anew for patients, even though the number of beds never exceeded 5–6 throughout the 18th century. The important clinical and anatomical demonstrations were resumed and new disciplines such as surgery and obstetrics were encouraged (which aroused indignation in certain quarters—should such theses as "On abortion", "On impotence" be ventilated at the University?). Rosén was an industrious author of textbooks; he wrote a handbook on anatomy and another on childhood diseases which, after translation into numerous languages, became a classic in paediatrics. Whilst improvements in teaching continued, academic requirements were raised and conferment of degrees in medicine became a regular feature. For the very first time, a Swedish undergraduate could complete his entire medical training in his own country.

Surgery had for long been a profession with a low status. Surgeons were usually only cursorily trained barbers or military barber-surgeons, but after a time their role was taken over by physicians. In 1744 the University was accorded its first chair in anatomy and surgery and Adolf Murray was the first to be appointed. He was equally well known for the high demands he placed on his students as for his advanced anatomical preparations. Eighteenth century surgery was less hampered by technical deficiencies than by the complicating problem of infected sores and wounds. There was in addition the lack of satisfactory anaesthetics. Simply put, one can say that 18th century surgery was concentrated on four types of operation: amputation, trepanation (opening of the skull), urolithotomy (operation for stone in the urinary bladder), and cataract operations.

NATURAL HISTORY—CARL VON LINNÉ

The most eminent personality without exception in Swedish 18th century science was Carl von Linné (otherwise known as Linnaeus). After his years spent in Holland as a young botanical genius, Linné took up the professorship in theoretical medicine with botany and zoology in 1741. Instruction in natural history at Uppsala had been sadly neglected. Even Linné himself had never during his student days received a single lesson in botany, while in zoology, all that had been offered was the younger Rudbeck's lectures on birds. The University's natural history collection in the Gustavianum had nothing more to show than a few ossified small animals and one or two curiosities.

Linné soon elevated Swedish natural history to heights that attracted world-wide attention. In complete accord with the

Carl von Linné.

Hat Party's industrial policy and with a view to the public good, Linné made a methodical inventory of the animal, vegetable and mineral kingdoms. His journeys throughout Sweden on behalf of Parliament are well-known, and even today make lively reading. In the Botanical Garden he grew medicinal herbs. The Garden was a base from which he encouraged his students to introduce and cultivate a variety of useful plants. However, neither the tea bush nor the cotton plant would thrive, though the potato did well, as is known.

Since the time of Olof Rudbeck the Elder the botanical garden in Svartbäcken had been allowed to grow wild. The beds were now partly overgrown and the prefectorial residence was uninhabitable. When Linné became professor, the University went to the expense of building an orangery, restoring the residence and carrying out a thorough remodelling of the gardens in the strict French fashion. The most significant improvement concerned of course the actual plant collection. At first Linné laboriously gathered and begged both seeds and growing plants, but in pace with his spreading fame, contributions streamed in from disciples and botanists all over the world. In just a few years the number of plants was increased from 200 to about 3,000. Linné even collected around him live zoological exhibits, in the form of a small menagerie: a few monkeys, a couple of raccoons and a variety of exotic birds. For each individual animal the University made a special maintenance allowance; thus the raccoons were allotted nine öre per day for the pair to live on.

The 1760's were literally the palmy days of the Botanical Garden. It was pre-eminent in all of Europe as regards number of species and constituted one of the country's greatest sights. Yet another attraction was the collection of natural history exhibits—preserved mammals, birds, fishes, insects, etc.—

Linné was the first to include the human being in a zoological system. He placed him in the Homo family among the hominoids and called him Homo sapiens. A representation of the hominoids in descending scale from Homo sapiens. From Linné's Antropomorpha *(1760).*

housed in the Orangery. Like the herbs, this collection grew quickly. Royal personages, East India traders and others donated whole private collections; to bequeath one's collection to Linné was considered an honour!

All these animals, even the larger ones such as monkeys, armadillos and otters, were conserved in spirit during Linné's time, but later reconserved by taxidermy. Of the original collection, which was widely representative, only a few examples remain. Nevertheless the material is still of considerable zoological interest as it contains several typological examples of Linné's species descriptions in the innovative tenth edition of *Systema naturae.* By means of a deceptively simple division into six classes, Linné created a firm basis for all zoological research.

He was the first to place Man in a zoological taxonomy, regarding the human being as one species of the Homo family among the apes and therefore applied the name *Homo sapiens.*

Linné's main subject was and remained botany. He was the systematist, the arranger who brought order to the boundless wealth of the plant world by applying his principles of classification, as ingenious as they were simple. In his little book *Blommornas biläger* (Floral Nuptuals) of 1729, Linné had already asserted the existence of sexuality in the plant world, in other words that they propagate by fertilization by means of stamens and pistils as sexual organs. The concept was not new, yet created an enormous sensation.—"the manuscripts flew around among the students".

In his pioneering *Systema naturae* (1735), Linné established that plant sexuality could constitute the basis for a completely new systematics. Here he distributed the plants into classes and rankings, using the number of stamens and pistils as their distinguishing characteristic. In this way he created a clear and readily comprehended scheme where all plants could be classed and found. It was just this simplicity that was the system's strength and which allowed it soon to oust all other, older systems, less easy to comprehend.

The first edition of *Systema naturae* comprised only 14 folio pages, but then it does not attempt to describe each individual species; rather, it sets out the basic principles for the classification. It was prepared and printed in Holland and soon became known on the Continent. It was to be the foundation-stone for Linné's subsequent world renown. New editions followed, one after another; right from the start the comprehensive systematics included also the animal and mineral kingdoms. Between the first edition and the last, the twelfth, over 2,000 pages were added.

doned his lectures at the rostrum to lead botanical rambles in the environs of Uppsala. The numbers joining these excursions were truly amazing. Sometimes Linné would be surrounded by as many as 200 students, many in uniform and equipped with butterfly nets, vascula, and pins with which to attach flowers and butterflies to their hats. They would start out from one or other of the town gates at eight in the morning and during the day made halts when they examined and compared their trophies, whilst Linné informed them about the structure and names of their specimens, their practical uses and their importance in folklore. Towards dusk they returned to Uppsala with music and song and Linné was accompanied to the Prefectorial Residence where he was thanked with cheers. These excursions had become legendary even during Linné's own lifetime.

Today only fragments of Linné's own collections and his books and manuscripts are preserved in Sweden. After the death of Linné's son Carl, the property was put up for sale to the highest bidder and sold in 1784 to an English private collector after the Swedish state had put in only a halfhearted bid. The collections are now held in trust by the Linnean Society in London. The national loss may be regarded as great, but it has been claimed, with justification, that the materials have been far better cared for than they would have been in their homeland.

But the Linnean heritage was firmly established. Among the students who sat at his feet in Uppsala were many who became clergymen, who carried with them a deep-seated interest in Nature out to vicarages all over Sweden. Many were rural vicars who gratefully made good use of this proof of God's infinite wisdom and creativity offered by Nature, and who enriched their everyday lives by collecting herbs and insects and lovingly classifying them in true Linnean manner.

Another type of Linnean disciple achieved greater fame—those who travelled to far-off lands in search of exotic flora and fauna and to collect rare specimens of the natural world. It is difficult today to conceive of the hardships with which the scientific explorers of those days had to contend. Many of his disciples succumbed, never to return to their homeland. We can mention Peter Forsskål who journeyed to Arabia, where clad as a Bedouin, he wandered over vast areas, only to have his collections confiscated and himself die of malaria. Another was Anders Sparrman who made his way to the Cape of Good Hope and eventually accompanied the legendary James Cook to the South Pacific; he brought home with him enormous quantities of items of natural history or of ethnographic interest. Carl Peter Thunberg journeyed to Japan where during 15 intensive months he charted the whole of that country's unknown flora. His *Flora Japonica* (1784) has been described as a pioneer achievement, not least by the Japanese themselves. Thunberg was the one who most tangibly passed on the Linnean heritage. In 1784 he succeeded to the Linnean professorship and his life's work was to administer and classify the University's huge collections of natural history exhibits, which he complemented with his own. It was he who designed the new botanical gardens below Uppsala Castle and who, at the inauguration of the Linnean Hall in 1807, spoke in lofty tones of Linné who had reformed botany as a discipline and who had caused the name of Sweden to "fly out over the world".

TEACHING

No great changes were made in the University's organisation during the 18th century. The Constitutions of 1655 remained unchanged right up to the mid-19th century. The University succeeded for the most part in averting parliamentary demands for a more professionally oriented education. The only new feature was the so-called civil examinations which were introduced in the mid-18th century for posts in any branch of the Civil Service.

Superficially, the educational curriculum continued as before. The Senate House and the restored Gustavianum offered new and improved premises. Each professor lectured four days a week, with private tutorials inbetween to supplement their rather lean salaries. The doctoral disputations and the annual examinations made a break in the regular daily university life. The conferment of Masters' degrees every third year were magnificent occasions, with much music and oratory in Latin, while the ladies were regaled with sweets and liqueurs, so as not to suffer too much boredom.

Despite the forceful advances of natural science and research, the theological and humanistic disciplines held firm. However, the antagonism between the natural sciences and theology which had triggered the Cartesian battles had now abated somewhat, not least because the natural scientists themselves often adopted a specially religious stance, that of so-called physiotheology, according to which everything in Nature is so purposefully created that it could only be explained as the work of an omniscient deity. Everything, from the microscopic life in a drop of water, the remarkable properties of electrical energy, to the passage of the stars across the heavens, proved the existence of God. The latest findings of natural science merely served to confirm the fundamental theological concepts.

Theology still attracted one-third of the entire student population. Knowledge of the classical languages, especially Latin, was considered indispensable. Latin was by and large the natu-

Uppsala students according to drawings from 1737 and 1823.

ral language of education and the self-evident medium of the learned. Within philosophy, metaphysics was in decline, though the Wolffian battles in mid-century, as also the radical philosophy of the Enlightenment, kept the subject alive and well. The Skyttean professorship in politics and oratory was held for most of the epoch by Johan Ihre, who, with his comprehensive Swedish dictionary, was also a pioneer in Nordic philology.

Yet it was the natural scientists who were now in the limelight. Unobtrusively, they were adding a new dimension to education. Bent over the model of a plough in the Theatrum oeconomicum, watching with bated breath demonstrations in experimental physics or chemistry—or during the legendary Linnean herbarial lectures—students were experiencing something completely new. Where the dry schoolroom lectures had made an abstraction of Nature, here it was staged and illustrated before their eyes. For the first time, their teacher stood beside them and demonstrated his knowledge in practical terms.

One might have expected the student population to have increased steeply during this period when the University's renown was at its zenith, and when the population of the country rose from 1.4 million in 1720 to 2.3 million by 1800. Yet, inexplicably, the student population declined from about 1,000 at the beginning of this period, to reach a record low of about 450 in the 1780's. The reason may lie in part in the social restructuring of Swedish society which slowly occurred during the 18th century. The proportion of clergymen's sons decreased, while the growing bourgeois class was not yet providing a particularly large source of recruitment. By contrast, the proportion of farmers' sons remained about 20% throughout the century, even at that time quite a high figure compared with other countries.

The Era of Student Song and Jubilation

c. 1800–1880

The spirit of the times underwent a change during the Gustavian reign. The purposeful utilitarian politics were on the retreat—they had failed to accomplish the great transformation of Sweden that the statesmen had hoped for. Now instead opened the era of a French-inspired taste for Belles-Lettres, art, theatre and literature. Sweden's cultural centre was no longer Uppsala, but Stockholm.

Politically speaking, Gustav III's reign (1772–1792) was an uneasy, anxious time. The antagonism between royalty and nobility sharpened with the passing years and with the murder of the King in 1792 (later to serve as the theme of the opera *The Masked Ball*), it appeared that the nobility had got their revenge for having been deprived of important privileges. Gustav had pitted the commoners' interests against those of the nobility. But this was a double-edged move—a gamble taken to prevent at all costs the ideas of the French Revolution from gaining a foothold in Sweden. During the reign of Gustav IV Adolf (1792–1809), fear of the revolutionary dreams of freedom and equality continued to mount. Gustav suspected revolt and treachery at every turn. The students at Uppsala were among those who would feel the consequences of this.

As a corporate body, the students had hitherto not had much

71

to say, but, stimulated by the talk of liberty heard from France, they plucked up courage for the first time to declare themselves as a group with independent opinions and demands. One deciding factor was that to an ever increasing extent students were coming from the homes of the economically important middle class. By showing their interest in culture and education, they wanted to legitimize their influential role in public life. In the state institutions and the professions, academic qualifications had become increasingly important since in 1789 Gustav III had abolished the sole right of the nobility to the high offices of state. The student population now increased steeply and the mixing of citizens from different estates in society also increased appreciably, and a marked shift in the proportions of students from the different estates took place. For the first time, the students could create their own status in society, without needing to belong to the upper class.

With a new sense of confidence and fully conscious of their role as men of the future, the students were particularly susceptible to the ideas and trends that were in the air. Movements such as romantic idealism, royalism, Scandinavianism and, later, liberalism, were quick to catch on in the student world. The students therefore found themselves cast firmly in the role of creators of cultural and political opinion. At the same time student-life took on a fuller and more organized form. A calendar of festivities was devised which had a profound effect on student social life. Singers and authors created a student romanticism that made students immeasurably popular everywhere. Both within and outside the University, the period around the middle of the 19th century was in great part the heyday of student life.

RADICAL STUDENTS

The entry of the students onto the political stage can be directly attributed to the French Revolution. Events in France aroused great enthusiasm in some quarters even here in Sweden; in Stockholm, rumour was rife that the Uppsala students wore the cockade of freedom and drank toasts to the Revolution. Libertarian ideas went hand in hand with the growing dissatisfaction with the despotic use of royal power. Gustav IV Adolf had curtailed liberty of the press in 1792 and this triggered the first open protests; in one daring demonstration, the students tramped through the streets in a mock funeral cortège before ceremonially interring press liberty. This was followed by the customary funeral feast. The following day a few "mourners" gathered to form the so-called Convention, knowing full well that the name would immediately be associated with the National Convention which had recently proclaimed the French Republic and executed Louis XVI. In Stockholm, the King was both affronted and enraged, and not a little frightened at this turn of events. On his state visit to Uppsala in March 1793 he came protected by a strong military escort. In a royal decree a month later he banned the Convention and forbade all large gatherings of students.

Thus the students were forced to seek new ways to express their discontent. Radicalism found a platform in the so-called Junta, a little coterie which under the guise of occupying itself with music and literature, actually engaged in the inflammatory politics of the day. Its leader was the philosopher Benjamin Höijer, already in disgrace and methodically opposed because of his general radicalism, and in addition, G. A. Silfverstolpe and Hans Järta—all men who later played a large part in the change of regime of 1809, when Gustav Adolf was deposed and

Uppsala students demonstrating. From a French newspaper, 1857.

forced into exile. The Junta became the source of unrest, with renewed demonstrations against the King's increasingly reactionary policies. Events culminated about the turn of the century, at a time when Napoleon Bonaparte stood at the peak of his popularity, while Gustav Adolf allied himself with the detested Russian monarchy. Gustav's coronation in 1800 presented a golden opportunity for demonstrations of disapproval. In Uppsala the event was to be celebrated with orations and ceremonial music. The Junta were not slow to exploit the occasion to poke fun at the contemptible monarchists; they even succeeded in smuggling some French revolutionary printed music into the coronation celebrations, though the plan was scotched at the last minute and the music was removed from the programme. The students then protested in their turn by leaving the banqueting hall and marching through the streets, singing the Marseillaise. The scandal was now complete. The sequel was a lengthy trial, the so-called Music Case, heard before the Senate and leading to severe sentences. Several Junta members were dismissed from their posts and expelled from the University. For the moment, student opposition was effectively crushed.

AFTER 1809—ROYALISM AND GOTHIC ROMANTICISM

After 1809, the revolutionary mood was forgotten. That the antagonism between the students and those in power waned can be attributed in part to the arrival in Uppsala of German idealist philosophy, though this was itself initially regarded as revolutionary. Even the Junta's men had applauded the German philosopher, Kant, as the liberator of human thought, just

75

as the French Revolution had liberated fettered French society.

On the political front, idealism emphasized the overriding role of the state, in the name of national unity. All citizens had to show allegiance to the state, whose interests were paramount in all things. A conservative ideology began to permeate the University: the Revolution of 1809 had proved futile and merely caused unrest and anarchy; now was the time to close ranks around national values and raise them above crass materialistic ambition. Vanished was all desire to oppose. Now it was the students who formed the vanguard in enthusiastic support of the heir apparent, Karl Johan, Napoleon's former general, Jean Baptiste Bernadotte. The new watchwords were nationalism, royalism, idealism. The Gothic spirit was once more stirred into life, just as liable now as during the Great Power Era, to arouse patriotic feelings.

The student ovations that met members of the Royal House on their frequent visits to Uppsala during the first decades of the 19th century may today appear a trifle fantastic. The paying of homage in song, turgid speechmaking and handshaking succeeded one another. The heady days of Swedish history set the tone and the Gothic symbols were recreated. Surrounded by hundreds of students, the royal guests wended their way to Old Upsala, where they climbed the famous burial mounds from Viking times, sang Gothic ballads and drank mead from the symbolic horn.

A prize example of such fanciful royalism was the celebration of the 'nameday' of Crown Prince Oscar in 1819. The students wanted to turn the day into a gigantic manifestation of true Swedish nationalism. The original plan was to hold the ceremony on the tumuli at Gamla Upsala—torch-bearing students would transform the mounds into prehistoric sacrificial pyres and the old church would be illuminated by an enormous fiery cross, while the Crown Prince, borne aloft on a shield, would accept "the reverences and cries of delight of the commoners, forgathered on the heath". But the plan went awry and the ceremony was staged instead in the yard of the Gustavianum, where a temple had been constructed in Gothic style. Carried past close on a thousand torch-bearing and singing students, the Prince was placed on the throne of the temple and there received their gifts—a sword and a horn of frothy mead. Next the Prince girded on the sword and drained the mead horn to the accompaniment of noisy Gothic martial music. The populace was carried away with enthusiasm. "Everywhere on this wonderful evening, one saw how every soul was filled with but two ideas: the fatherland and the royal dynasty which loves its light and protects its freedom" (Atterbom, Swedish poet, subsequently Professor of Philosophy and, later, also of Aesthetics in Uppsala).

SCANDINAVIANISM

Yet the tide turned once again. Beginning in the 1830's, a new wave of growing liberalism began to make headway against the conservative ideals. Once again it was students who formed the vanguard; the liberal newspaper *Aftonbladet* was read with fervour. Foreign affairs and King Karl Johan's friendly attitude toward the Russians stirred up opposition on the domestic front and scandalized student demonstrations once again captured the press headlines. Hand in hand with the new political orientation went a reaction against the romantic idealism that had made Uppsala a bastion of conservatism. The conversion of Erik Gustaf Geijer, Professor of History and Vice-Chancellor of the University, to Liberalism was greeted with jubilation as a gesture of freedom.

From the Student Meeting of 1875. Students gather round the Nordic banner with its academic laurel crown in a spirit of Scandinavianism.

During the 1840's, the Golden Age of the students and student life, the political undercurrents broke out into open hostilities. The students were to play a conspicuously significant political role by their involvement in the powerful wave of Scandinavianism that arose at the time. This had its origin in Denmark; in the face of the German threat to the Duchies of Schlesvig and Holstein, the liberal students there looked to their Scandinavian neighbours for support. It was a matter of making Denmark's cause appear to be that of all the Nordic countries and to create a strong sense of unity.

The Swedish students were immediately enthused by the idea. The first united demonstrations were held in 1843. Two hundred advocates of Scandinavianism descended on Uppsala, where they received a riotous welcome from the students. Several grand receptions were held under the banner of brotherhood; all were agreed—Denmark's cause was also our concern. Despite strong opposition from King Karl Johan, whose Russophilic politics were threatened by the concept of Nordic Union, student meetings continued by turns in the Scandinavian towns. Their tone became increasingly aggressive and soon turned against the traditional foe, imperial Russia. The French February Revolution of 1848 inflamed student feelings even more. It was at this juncture that the Danish-German War broke out. In a huge demonstration, the Uppsala students pledged their Danish brothers—and all other freedom lovers—their loyal support. By this time, the Scandinavian libertarian ethos had gained ground in all classes of society, not least among the royalty, which set ambitious hopes on a Nordic Union. Thus the political aspirations of the students now coincided with those of the State. Student meetings continued throughout the 1850's and 1860's, but their increasingly regularized and established forms had a cooling effect on the original fervour. In 1863–64, the renewed Danish-German War ended in catastrophe. Despite the lofty promises of support and assistance, Denmark was left to fight, single-handed, a hopeless battle.

Though Scandinavianism thus ended in defeat, the students had at least shown by it that they were a force to be reckoned with as creators of public opinion. The ideas ventilated at student meetings came to be embraced by all politically influential classes in the Nordic countries. Student Scandinavianism played a significant role in the development of Scandinavian cooperation in innumerable areas of social life and has done so right down to the present.

UPPSALA AND ROMANTICISM

The increasing importance of the University as an institution for the education of future civil servants added to student self-esteem. According to idealistic philosophy the state was considered a spiritual and organic entity, and in order to equip oneself to serve that state, it was necessary to gain a comprehensive understanding of its principles and functioning. It was the University that supplied that knowledge.

The students were nurtured with this ideology to form a consciousness of their own importance. The intention was to manifest in various ways the importance of students as a group within society, as the future guardians of society. It was with an awareness of this inheritance, and under the influence of Scandinavianism, that the students formed themselves into a corporate body in 1849. The typical student now took form—white-capped, punch-tippling, witty, and boldly conscious of his role

Students serenading, 1869.

6 – A Life of Learning

as a man of the future. Students were amazingly and widely popular. Another factor that enhanced their popularity was their elaborate calendar of feasts and the creation of the strong tradition of student song. Gunnar Wennberg's *Gluntarne*, a more intimate sort of student song portraying the classic life of the student, is a living tradition even today.

About this time, the barriers between the University and bourgeois society began to disintegrate. The old class divisions could no longer be either justified or upheld against the influx of middle class students; democratic social intercourse was an inevitable consequence. At about this time too, many of the nobility moved in to the towns from their country estates. Uppsala was a favourite because of the accessibility there of cultural life and spiritual enlightenment, and where it was natural to meet with teachers and students. Parlours in private dwellings became meeting places for erudite conversations, music-making and literary improvisations. In this setting, it was talent and not extraction that counted. If a country student could but write poetry, recite, or play an instrument, he was made welcome.

The parlours drew intellectual sustenance from the Romantic movement, originally imported from Germany. In Sweden, Romanticism spread from Uppsala, where Geijer, Atterbom and others, all University personalities, were the foremost advocates. 1810 saw the publication of the ideological pamphlet *Phosphoros*, followed a year later by *Poetisk kalender* (Poetic Directory). Romantic idealism prevailed at the University throughout the first half of the 19th century. But on this very account, the University was to be accused of being a stronghold of reaction, lacking contact with the real world.

The genuine Romantic valued only the eternal truths raised above human corruptibility and crass materialism. The Good,

82

the True, the Beautiful were the real objectives of true science. Hence it followed that the exact sciences were consigned to the background and in their place the humanities received pride of place: history, philosophy, literature and aesthetics.

The doyen of Romanticism at Uppsala was, until his apostasy, Erik Gustaf Geijer, lionized as historian and author, beloved of students and of parlour devotees. He was the personification of all the foremost trends of the time. His view of history was idealistic, based on the concept of the nation as a living organism, united by its common history and destiny. As a lecturer, Geijer was exceedingly popular and society audiences jostled with students around his lectern in the Gustavianum. The atmosphere was charged. "Geijer lectured in such a manner that I can scarcely imagine it possible for anything more splendid to issue from a human soul. The hall was crammed. All was silent as the grave. None there was who listened dry-eyed or whose heart did not pound." Geijer himself often refrained from concealing his emotion when painting his grandiose visions or recalling God's monumental works. It is quite understandable that his defection to liberalism should have aroused such consternation.

This exaggerated emotionalism is otherwise even more closely associated with Atterbom. He it was who led Uppsala Romanticism, at first far more daringly provocative than the Senate could tolerate. A scandalously erotic poem aroused a reaction against the seduction of dangerous Romanticism and after further outspoken statements, Atterbom was threatened with expulsion from the University. Yet, despite strong opposition within certain quarters of the University, he was appointed Professor of Philosophy in 1828. A few years later, he transferred to the newly created Chair of Aesthetics and Modern Literature, so typical of its time. But Atterbom never became a truly popular figure. Moreover his poetry was far too mawkish and his scholarship far too intricately prolix. After Geijer's defection, Atterbom became increasingly care-worn and isolated. The students now looked upon him as a slightly strange character, the symbol of obsolete ideals.

For the Romantics the most important subject was philosophy. The popular Benjamin Höijer, with a past in the Junta (cf. p. 73), and therefore persecuted for his radicalism, eventually received a well-deserved professorship in 1809, three years before his death. He developed his own, independent form of German idealistic philosophy and came to play a decisive role as ideologist for the Uppsala Romantics. His successors Nils Fredrik Biberg and Sigurd Ribbing guided the originally radical German philosophy into calmer, safer waters. A highlight of Uppsala idealism was reached with Christopher Jacob Boström (Professor of Applied Philosophy, 1842–63), according to whom the material world exists only as Divine properties. The earthly had actually no reality outside the consciousness of Man. According to one of the many anecdotes in the rich flora surrounding Boström, the student who responded to the examination question "is the stove that the undergraduate is now gazing at outside or within him?" with the answer "outside" was promptly failed! The eternal truths could only be sought behind the trivialities of reality. Boström came to exercise a considerable, if hard to define, influence, not least on the training given to Civil Servants during the final decades of the 19th century.

THE NATURAL SCIENCE OF ROMANTICISM

Whereas the historical and philosophical sciences now occupied the centre of the stage, the natural sciences were confined to the wings. From a narrow Romantic point of view, objective natural research could appear to be more or less trivial. Some went even further—they even held the opinion that science denied all spiritual values and encouraged vulgar materialism. The Romantics dominated the scene by virtue of their highly effective propaganda. Such disciplines as physics and chemistry went into eclipse during the first half of the 19th century, with insufficient instruction and research. It was a sign of the times that the royal visits to the laboratories ceased. No longer was it experiments in chemistry and physics that excited wonder: instead it was the lectures of Geijer, Atterbom and Boström that drew the crowds.

That a science such as botany could so readily be combined with the ideals of Romanticism was nothing to wonder at. The mysteries of life and the perfection of the plant world spontaneously invited profound speculation. Added to this was the Linnéan tradition, whose far-reaching influence can scarcely be overestimated. It was during the era of Romanticism that the image of Linné as a national saint was created. It is significant that it was just botany that received the only new University premises to be built during the first half of the 19th century. It was in 1807 that a royal donation by Gustav III financed the building of the large Linnéan Hall, with adjoining greenhouse in the new botanical gardens below the Castle. These were executed in neoclassical style, which was an abrupt departure from other University buildings. The effect was entirely intentional. The new Botanicum was to resemble a temple, dedicated to elaborate lectures in the spirit of the great Linné.

In the person of Elias Fries, later to become internationally known for his important contributions within mycology, botany gained an advocate fully worthy of the great ideals of Romanticism. For him it was primarily a question of interpreting Nature

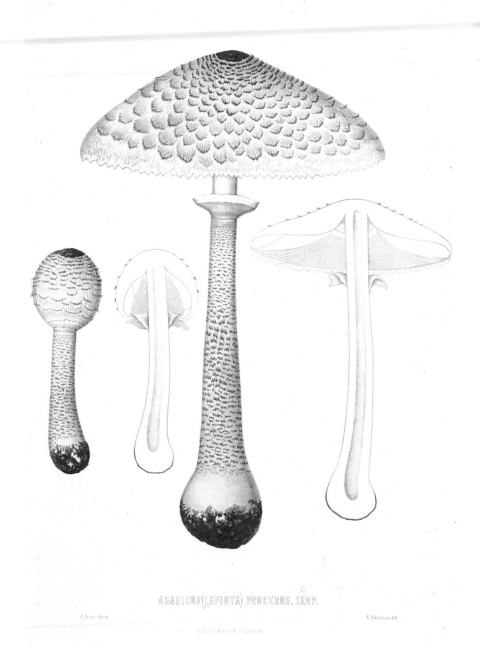

AGARICUS(LEPIOTA) PROCERUS. SKOP.

E.Price direx   E.Pettersson del

Lith.och tr hos A.J.Salmson

as a reflection of the Divine spirit; neither the magnifying glass nor the microscope was his instrument, but rather the "love of God".

Medicine too found favour under the guidance of Israel Hwasser, appointed Professor in 1830. Hwasser exemplifies how Romantic philosophy and the natural sciences could be united. For him the important thing was not specialization, or crass utilitarian know-how. All sciences derive from the same Divine source, and so must always be. Medicine was in his view essentially a philosophical science. His great but shocking thesis was *Sickness is Self-destruction (Sjukdom är självförstöring)*. Since disease is self-inflicted, it could in Hwasser's opinion be healed only by Divine intervention. The role of the physician was to prepare the way for and aid the healing process; his moral or religious task was just as important as were the practical measures.

That such views were less acceptable outside Uppsala is understandable. From Stockholm, the authoritative and world-famous chemist, Jöns Jacob Berzelius, proposed that medical education in its entirety should be transferred to the newly founded Karolinska Institute. However, an indignant Hwasser succeeded in having the proposal quashed; to transfer the medical faculty would be to destroy the unity that the University constituted.

Nevertheless the seed had been sown and the idea of moving the University spread, especially in liberal circles in Stockholm, where accusations were levelled at Uppsala University as lacking any contact with reality, while at the same time calls were made for practical utilitarianism—just as during the Great Power era and the Period of Liberty: the University must place itself at the service of society and promote practical and economic advance. The attacks culminated around 1860 in the liberal newspaper *Aftonbladet:* the University fostered nothing but "imbecilic dreamers or conceited and intolerant pedants". The only remedy was to transfer all activities to Stockholm, where the enforced proximity to reality would puncture academic narcissism.

But the vehemence of the liberal onslaught was misleading, for the University was safely anchored in Uppsala. There it could effectively continue to play its part as an institution for the training of civil servants; there was never any real danger to its continued existence. Bye and bye the criticisms died down when the liberal forces saw that their demands had been met by the founding during the 1870s of the Royal Institute of Technology and Stockholm University.

The image of an otherworldly, "ivory tower" university moreover is seen to correspond very poorly to the relatively rapid development that took place within the natural science disciplines during the second half of the 19th century. In 1852 a professorship in zoology was created and the following year the professorship in chemistry was divided into two, one for general and agricultural chemistry and another for mineralogy. That year too the title of the old chair in dietetics, botany and *materia medica* was altered to medical and physiological chemistry and finally in 1873 yet another professorial chair in the natural sciences was created, that of mechanics. Among the scientists of that period we find such great names as Gustaf Svanberg in astronomy, Lars Fredrik Svanberg (no relation) in chemistry, and Knut Ångström in physics. It also became common for lecturers to be recruited from the technical institutes in Stockholm.

ASTRONOMY, PHYSICS AND CHEMISTRY

The natural sciences received new premises. First to be favoured was astronomy, whose old observatory had long been obsolescent. The new observatory was inaugurated in 1853. For its time it was a lavishly equipped and exceedingly functional installation. With its characteristic architecture it was regarded as a symbol not only for progressive astronomy but also for a new era of scientific investigation. "The great, mobile cupola... like a mirror of silver reflected the sun's rays and even at two leagues' distance aroused amazement in those approaching the town. It was thought to be some sort of magic." Many new instruments were procured for the observatory, not least a large refracting telescope in 1861, which marked the transition within astronomical research from movable to fixed instrumentation.

Physics too had been beset with problems during the first half of the 19th century, but with the accession in 1858 of Anders Jonas Ångström as professor, the situation changed considerably. He introduced practical experiments and saw to it that physics as a discipline was housed for the first time in its own premises: a lecture hall and several smaller rooms over the newly built chemistry laboratory. This was the first time students had access to the Department's instruments and apparatus and the opportunity to carry out experiments themselves. At this time, Ångström was one of the internationally best known scientists at the University. His main field was optical spectral analysis. He succeeded in determining the spectrum of a series of metals and alloys and also formulated the so-called law of absorption which states that a body can absorb the same type of light that it will transmit when glowing. Another important achievement was Ångström's analytical measurements of the solar spectrum which were published towards the end of the 1860s in *Recherches sur le spectre solaire*. He prepared an atlas of the solar spectrum with information on wavelengths for a thousand or so lines. For many years the atlas was the main standard for the determination of wavelengths; the linear unit introduced by Ångström, one ten-millionth of a millimetre, was called after its inventor and established internationally in 1905.

Even such a discipline as chemistry, regarded by the most sarcastic Romantics with a goodly measure of disdain, could look towards a much brighter future around the middle of the century. By that time the centre for Swedish chemistry had long been Stockholm and the Academy of Sciences, with Berzelius as its internationally respected celebrity. But even in Uppsala the discipline made headway after Berzelius' pupil, Svanberg, had been appointed professor. Svanberg was determined that a new chemistry laboratory should be built and in 1859 the largest single academic building at the University stood ready for use, an imposing and well equipped chemical centre, sited in the so-called English Park. The premises were also intended to house other subjects within the natural sciences.

MEDICINE

In the person of the idealist Hwasser the medical faculty had had an energetic advocate, but as regards its financial resources it was less well served. The number of beds at the University Hospital (Nosocomium academicum) was barely a dozen at the beginning of the 19th century. However, when in 1831 the University received its first state grant, the hospital was allocated 5,000 riksdaler for general improvements plus a small annual allowance for running expenses. The number of beds was increased to 40, of which eight were for students, free of charge, financed by a special levy on all students at the beginning of each term. In the 1850s the University Hospital and the County Hospital were amalgamated, giving a total of around 100 beds; at the County Hospital, next to the Gustavianum, surgical and venereal cases were attended to, while medical cases were the province of the old University Hospital.

This new regime meant that the premises were filled to bursting-point; they were overcrowded and the hygienic situation left much to be desired. There was thus an acute need for new, modern premises. The town and county authorities along with the University succeeded in a combined effort in scraping together the necessary capital and in 1867 the new University Hospital could be commissioned. The number of beds now rose to 171 and this also made it possible to give broad clinical instruction.

Another factor that contributed to a broadening of medical training was the new departments that were built during the 1850s and 1860s for the disciplines anatomy, physiology and pathology. The anatomical department stood ready in 1850. From this time on, students were obliged to carry out dissections, even though under rather primitive conditions. There was no heating and lighting consisted of a few simple gas lamps. During the 1870s, however, what came to be called the last macroanatomical discovery was made at the department. The student Ivar Sandström found during a routine dissection of a dog an organ of unknown appearance, lying just above the thyroid glands. This was the so-called parathyroid gland whose existence he could confirm after a comprehensive empirical investigation.

The premises for physiology and pathology were ready for occupation in 1867, thanks to a donation from the private benefactor, Anders Fredrik Regnell. The physiological laboratory was the first in Scandinavia. Here too, obligatory laboratory training was introduced for the students in the 1870s. Professor Frithiof Holmgren, subsequently an active sympathizer with the radical students, was an eccentric but inventive character. He was one of Sweden's first Darwinists and conducted important research within the modern physiology of the senses. His investigations into colour blindness, prompted by the idea that a puzzling railway accident in 1875 might have been the consequence of the locomotive driver's colour blindness, has been of great practical importance. Holmgren himself tramped the entire distance between Uppsala and Gävle (some 100 km by rail) on a rail trolley and investigated with simple means (rag dolls, signal flags, etc.) the colour vision of railway personnel. A practical consequence of all this was the introduction of obligatory colour vision tests for all traffic personnel both on the railways and at sea. A few years later the method had been introduced in most European countries.

EDUCATION AND UNIVERSITY LIFE

Despite the vociferous threats of the liberal reform enthusiasts, the University stood firm. 1852 brought new statutes, but the only radical change was the abolition of the University's own jurisdiction. The first state grant, voted by Parliament in 1830, resulted in considerable changes. For 200 years the University had been obliged to get by as best it could on the proceeds of the Gustavian inheritance, then about 75,000 riksdaler annually. Now the State had all at once granted 24,000 riksdaler for "the perfecting of the University". The University authorities were of course overjoyed and in an atmosphere of profuse generosity they urged the various heads of departments and institutes to present their requests to the Senate.

During this period the number of professors increased from

92

The Book Hall in the University Library, Carolina Rediviva, inaugurated 1841.

24 to 52, and in addition there was an increase in the number of assistant lecturers and associate professors. During the same period the student population increased threefold, from about 500 to 1,500, though this took place intermittently. Even by mid-century the student population was still smaller than during the Great Power Era of the 17th century. A diminishing number were aiming to enter the ministry (20% by the close of this period), while increasing numbers were going in for an official career in the public services. For the first time, the faculty of law exceeded numerically the theological faculty.

As regards actual studies, all was as before. Lectures predominated; the 1820s and 1830s were their golden era. Students and socialites mixed in reverent admiration before the lectern when Geijer, Hwasser or Fries was to speak. The professors were not slow to adopt and exploit certain mannerisms. Of Hwasser, for example, it is said that before every lecture he rehearsed suitable gestures, while both Geijer and Fries were fond of closing their eyes and letting their voice quaver while declaiming particularly lofty passages. However, towards the middle of the century, interest in education waned, reaching a catastrophically low level by the 1860s and 1870s, when professors often had to lecture to audiences of four or five students! The lack of inspiration was mutual. The unpopularity of academic lectures was discussed keenly in the press: the problem seemed to be the difficulty of combining scientific content with elementary pedagogics. It was not until the introduction of teaching in seminars that the situation improved.

As regards examinations, the most far-reaching change took effect at the level of matriculation. Aspiring students had traditionally sat this examination at the University. It had long been customary for the Dean of the Faculty of Philosophy alone to conduct the examination, which meant that the requirements could often be arbitrary. For sons of the nobility and youths from well-to-do families the exam was generally a mere formality and it was not unknown for five- and six-year-old boys from privileged homes to be presented with a matriculation certificate. In 1831 the rules were amended so that the younger teachers of the Faculty of Philosophy conducted matriculation exams, each in his own subject. Right up to 1864, when the examinations were transferred to the state secondary grammar schools, sessions were held biannually at the Senate House, for well-known reasons called "Kuggis" (alluding jocularly to the numerous exam failures).

Student examination in the Senate House (Kuggis), mid-19th century.

As regards higher examinations, obligatory philosophical basic exams were introduced in the 1850s for those taking theology, medicine or jurisprudence, this being an expression of an old model for general education. The requirement for a written test in Latin remained, but Latin was no longer required for written theses and their public examination. That year too it was stipulated that the student must write his own dissertation—something that had previously not been self-evident.

Conferment of Masters' degrees took place only every third year, though with correspondingly greater pomp. After the ceremonial act in the Cathedral, followed dinner with guests in the botanical gardens and finally a ball in the grand Carolina

Conferment Dinner in the Botanical Gardens, 1869.

Hall, created in 1841 in the new library building Carolina Rediviva. The graduation was not now as it had been during the 17th century, a majestic and deeply serious affair, but was characterized by the gay, festive spirit brought by Romanticism to the University.

In 1877 the University celebrated its 400th anniversary in grandiose manner. King Oscar II was guest of honour and foreign guests could be counted by the hundred. The four-day celebrations consisted of a series of processions, speeches and banquets. One of the days was turned into a popular festival; fireworks and torchlight processions heightened the feeling of gaiety. The King, seated in a gilded throne, was borne through the cheering masses, while the town's poor were regaled with soup! The festivities culminated in the grand Act of Conferment in the Cathedral, where a cantata was performed, written by one of the most renowned Swedish bards of the day, Viktor Rydberg. His "Cantata for a Jubilee Graduation, 1877" formed a panagyric to the human pilgrimage through life, from darkness toward the light. The Jubilee was a gigantic celebration of the University as a spiritual centre in Swedish society. Its public relations value was enormous. Those critics who had called for the University's transfer were silenced once and for all.

The organizing committee responsible for arranging the 1877 Jubilee had put forward the suggestion for a new University building. The Gustavianum and the Senate House were both cramped and old-fashioned and the Carolina Hall in the library building was of course needed for its intended purpose. However, the project was slow to get started. Not until 1887 was the new University Building completed, on rising ground overlooking the Gustavianum, a palace in Renaissance style. The huge auditorium could hold 2,000. In addition there were stately

97

Entrance-hall in the new University House, inaugurated in 1887.

rooms for Senate and the Faculties and a series of lecture rooms in considerably simpler style. As the Danish literary historian and man of culture, Georg Brandes, expressed it on his visit to Uppsala in 1889: "Everything has been arranged to imbue youth with a wish to advance, a healthy ambition. Here everything exhorts the young: grow and rise and become a professor!".

The University Building can be regarded as the ultimate triumph of idealism in Uppsala. Its architecture, especially the magnificent auditorium, can be seen as an expression of an idealistic conception of the world. The ceiling in the auditorium represents the Absolute, from which one's gaze follows a natural downward course towards base matter—tangibly experienced in the hard, uncomfortable wooden benches. Above the entrance one can read an inscription taken from Thorild, the Swedish 18th century bard: "To think freely is great—but to think aright is greater". The citation was chosen for and aimed directly at those young radical students who had begun to shake up the old world of ideas, showing that the dawn of a new era was at hand.

Turning Towards Society

1880–1945

The period around 1880 was one of considerable unrest in Swedish society. Within several decades the population had risen from four to six million, industrialism had made its entry with accelerating pace and the growing working-class now threatened the safe position which the middle class had secured for itself during the first half of the 19th century. Socialist ideas were gaining ground, though the movement was not yet able to actively safeguard the workers' interests. Urbanization brought with it acute social problems. The old Parliament, comprised of the four estates—nobility, clergy, middle class and land-owners—and which had existed since the Middle Ages, was abolished in 1866, but the new two-chamber parliament betrayed the hopes for radical reforms. The aristocracy, the middle class and the land-owning farmers closed ranks to defend their privileges, while the working-class was still denied political representation.

In various ways the outside world thrust itself upon the University. Rhetorical idealism and much of the earlier conservative spirit was swept away, together with the fading, punch-tippling romanticism. It was time to choose sides and to take active part in the social debate. Such authors as the Swede Strindberg, the Dane Brandes and the Norwegian Ibsen, philosophers and political thinkers such as Comte and Marx—and especially Mill—were in vogue. Modern natural scientists, particularly Darwin, were making a profound impression. Progress and development were the watchwords of the day.

The new ideological currents not only helped alter the course of social development but also created a completely new intellectual climate, where students and teachers could gather to debate current affairs; belief in progress accorded the natural sciences a key role. It was with their help that development could be pushed ahead and all resources exploited for the general good. Industrialism increased the need for technical and scientific expertise. The development of the natural sciences that had commenced earlier in the 19th century was now accelerated; so too was the influx of students to the natural science departments.

SOCIALLY CONSCIOUS STUDENTS

The new radical ideas found a platform within the Liberal student society Verdandi, founded in 1882 on the initiative of the Liberal Karl Staaff and the Social-Democrat Hjalmar Branting. Their aim, taken from radical authors such as August Strindberg and Georg Brandes, was to submit problems to debate. Their programme also took up work with adult education and active support for workers' rights. The term "Verdandism" became synonymous with student radicalism. The public debates on ethical, social and political questions aroused enormous interest. This was a completely new and stimulating development in University life, that students and their teachers, on an equal footing, could give and take in a general discussion. In 1887 a debate on sexual morality aroused heated feelings and the introduction of such outspoken phrases as family planning, prostitution and extramarital liaisons was like

101

a slap in the face for bourgeois conventions. A storm broke out in the press and the Senate found itself obliged to intervene. Leading Verdandists were persecuted for several years.

Even so, the powers that be at the University no longer had the same means of applying pressure as a century earlier. Most Verdandists did well after their student years in Uppsala; one of them, Knut Wicksell, later became Professor in Political Economy and Finance in Lund, Karl Staaff became a minister in various Liberal governments and ultimately Prime Minister. Neither Frithiof Holmgren nor his successor Hjalmar Öhrvall was in any way threatened as holders of the Chair of Physiology.

Verdandi's most important role later became adult education. From the mid-1880's the society began to publish a series of popular scientific booklets, organized workers' libraries and art exhibitions and published articles and lectures in the daily press. Verdandi became a byword; its activities were a pioneering achievement in Swedish adult educational work.

One effect of Verdandi members' activities was that Conservative students also felt the need to organize themselves. The student society Heimdal was formed in 1891. It was a militant Conservative organization that immediately took up Verdandi's challenge by concentrating on adult education in the form of lectures, summer courses and the publishing of booklets and pamphlets. Third on the scene was the Social-Democratic student society Laboremus, founded in 1902.

Right from the start, Verdandi drew up the battle lines against Heimdal, but it was not until 1910 that the political antagonism between them became heated around the inflamed question of military defence. The Verdandists backed Karl Staaff's Liberal Government, whereas Heimdal members supported the Conservative opposition led by King Gustav V.

With the so-called Farmers March of 1914, when about 30,000 farmers took part, the right-wing appeared to have won the day. From Uppsala, Heimdal organized a Conservative show of strength; more than 1,000 students demonstrated their support for Gustav V by their presence at Stockholm Castle, the royal residence. In Uppsala the Verdandists were furious, alleging that the Heimdal demonstration had pretended to represent the opinion of the entire student population. On their return to Uppsala the Heimdalmen were met by hundreds of Verdandists, singing the Marseillaise. In a written statement to Staaff the left-wing students deprecated the Heimdal demonstration and avowed their continuing loyalty to the Government.

The political hostilities eventually led in 1915 to a stormy electoral campaign for Chairman of the Student Union, which was won by the Verdandi wing. After this the political front was quiet for a couple of decades when all collaborated instead in the common task of adult education.

In the mid-1930s, political storm clouds began to gather once more, driven by a right-wing wind. The controversy this time focused on the growing stream of Jewish refugees, which aroused concern among some students who feared competition on the labour market. In 1939 the Student Union gathered to decide on the matter. The meeting was one of the stormiest ever in the history of the Union. Eventually a resolution against granting entry permits to Jewish academics was passed by a large majority, despite opposition from both Verdandi and Laboremus. The resolution attracted much comment in the radical press and was interpreted as a victory for Nazi sympathies. The consequence was embarrassing for the Student Union, and all Nazi sympathizers were removed from leading positions.

Student life during the Second World War passed calmly

enough. The insistent realities of the outside world gave no scope for internal hostilities. Many students were drafted into the Armed Forces and the remainder worked together on actions in support of Finland, Norway and Denmark. On V.E. Day, 7th May 1945, celebrations were held all over Uppsala in the form of a gigantic extra Spring festival.

EDUCATION

Demands from the students for change, from the 1880s onwards, also included education. On all fronts they began to take an active part in the shaping of their education. They questioned the previous concepts of culture and the stultifying lectures; instead, students began to demand—and get—new, active forms of education. 1891 saw the introduction of obligatory seminars within all humanistic disciplines and the departments were made available for the students. At the same time, the first textbooks began to appear which established the requirements for various subjects within certain limits. Previously, each student examinee had been at the mercy of the professor's whims. The classic visit to the professor meant that the candidate, in formal dress, took himself off to his professor to learn what was expected of him. Then followed a hunt for senior students who could—or would—give hints and advice on questions and who might at a price sell their own compendiums. Certain basic texts, plus lecture notes, were the only course literature the student had access to.

Early in the 20th century changes were made in the examination system which meant the abolition, finally, of the old concept of an all-round education. The requirements for a bachelor's degree were lowered and new master's and "licenti-

The Professor and the Students. Cartoons from the beginning of the 20th century.

ate" degrees were introduced. (The "licentiate" degree required around four years of study after the master's degree, including a dissertation. This degree was roughly equivalent to the present-day *doktors examen*, Ph.D.) About 1910 the new educational system had been elaborated and would remain in use largely unchanged until the 1960s.

From 1,500 in 1880, the student population had swelled to almost 4,500 by 1945. As regards the composition of the intake, the trend persisted from the beginning of the 19th century onwards: the middle class formed the largest group, accounting for almost half of the students in 1914, while throughout the period the working-class was only minimally represented.

The greatest change in the recruitment population was that for the first time women were allowed entry to the University. The controversy surrounding women's right to education had kept pace with the number of middle class women lacking means of support. They were therefore regarded as a burden on society and ought consequently to have the right to some education. Thus the argument was a purely economic one. By mid-century, women were allowed to take, for example, lower posts within the postal and telegraph services and, somewhat later, to train for the teaching profession. In 1872 for the very first time, in all secrecy, a woman was admitted to the University. And in 1882 the first woman ever to defend a doctoral thesis at the University achieved this distinction; this was Ellen Fries (history). Gradually more and more women dared to follow, but the process was a slow one and even by the turn of the century the proportion of women to men was no higher than 2.7%. Many have witnessed to the trials and hardships these women students had to face during their years of study, often treated with contempt, and kept under constant scrutiny.

The big stumbling block was not; however, women's right to

Student feast at the turn of the century at Restaurant Rullan.

Dr Elsa Eschelsson was one of those women whose promotion was hindered by the wording of the Constitution that "Swedish meñ" were to be appointed to higher state posts. Not until 1923 was the formulation changed to "Swedish citizens".

university education *per se*, but their demand to be able to use it on the same footing as men. And for many this was unbearably presumptuous. A woman as university lecturer was just unthinkable—she could not possibly command the respect needed to foster *intellectual and moral development* and was in every way unsuited. What was more, it would be against the Constitution, which expressly spoke of the King's right to appoint "Swedish men" to public office.

The struggle of women to participate in public life has been a long and thorny one. Without doubt much of the opposition from male academics had its origin in their fear of competition on the labour market. It was only in 1923 that the wording of the Constitution was amended from "Swedish men" to "Swedish citizens" and only then could women as teachers assert themselves at the University.

HUMANISTIC RESEARCH IN THE SPIRIT OF ROMANTIC NATIONALISM

From the 1890s onwards, humanistic research came to be characterized by a spirit that contrasted sharply with the social climate and cultural radicalism prevailing in the preceding decade. The new era was one of romantic nationalism, a fervent national current nurtured by a strong feeling for Swedish popular culture and national identity. The trend was most evident in literature, where the concern with solving current problems prominent in the 1880s was superseded by a national individualism and aestheticism. The contrast was not, however, so profound as it might have appeared. Romantic nationalism did not stand in opposition to the natural sciences and itself contained a strong element of cultural pedagogics.

At the University, humanistic research stood at its zenith around 1900. The leading humanistic professors were influential moulders of opinion within the student world. The spirit of romantic nationalism gripped the students and for a time gave ideological support to the Conservative cause. One of these influential figures was the Professor of History, Harald Hjärne, whose research was based on the idealist tradition, though with an admixture of the new interest in source analysis and methodology. He was a brilliant debater and lecturer and the students flocked around him. "Historians of Hjärnes' school felt themselves to be a chosen band, and did not envy the other students, who had no genius as mentor but only mere professors" (Lydia Wahlström).

The prolific literary historian, Henrik Schück, preferred to devote himself to Swedish culture. So too did the Scandinavian philologist, Adolf Noreen, one of the founders of research into Swedish dialects. A lively debate was aroused by Noreen's radical and nationalistic spelling reform, which naturally won approval not least among the students. Other subjects that flourished in keeping with the spirit of the times were Nordic and classical archaeology and geography, all of which received their own chairs during the second decade. This wave of nationalist feeling reached a peak in the campaign to establish a professorship in the history of art; droves of students were enthused by the young lecturer, Johnny Roosval, to make a methodical inventory of all Sweden's churches in the search for forgotten art treasures. During that same decade, the history of art attained an unrivalled status in Uppsala and in 1917 was accorded the longed for professorial Chair.

Yet not all humanists were captivated by the notion of romantic nationalism. Axel Hägerström, Professor of Applied Philosophy from 1911, broke radically with everything tinged

A tutorial in Romance languages, 1891.

with idealism and 19th century sentiment. In contrast to Boström's philosophy, he claimed that it was only the world of
experience in time and space that actually existed. Within
moral philosophy he coined the term *värdenihilism* (value nihil-
ism), or the concept of the relativity of all things: there is no
such thing as good or evil; we cannot evaluate, but only analyse.
As a lecturer, Hägerström too had a strong influence on the
students. Terms such as *value nihilist* and *Hägerström-ist* became
epithets that were bandied about in debates on the philosophy
of life and about which all had to make up their minds. "Hägerström seemed in some remarkable way not only to be present in
conversations in student dens, but even in the very air itself",

according to one of the students of the time, the authoress Karin Boye.

Another of the mighty creators of opinion during the second and third decade of this century was Nathan Söderblom, humanist and theologian. Söderblom had been Professor of Theology since 1901, and was appointed Archbishop in 1915, after the Government had declared that it did not "dare" offer the students any other candidate than the immeasurably popular Söderblom. He was a brilliant speaker and shrewd analyst of the current situation, as a theologian undogmatic, always keeping in view the lofty ideal of ecumenism. His freedom from dogma made a deep impression on the Christian student movements of the day and also on the theological Faculty as a whole. It is significant that among conservative Christians, the Uppsala faculty was not considered to be altogether orthodox; they turned instead to Lund for clerical education in the traditional style.

NATURAL SCIENCES

In his Spring Speech of 1916, Nathan Söderblom spoke of Man's impotence before the technology he had called forth. With the horrors of the First World War now evident, there came the first doubts as to the self-evident rightness of the unrestrained expansion of technology and the natural sciences. Confidence in the future was shaken, progress was questioned. However, this debate scarcely affected research in Uppsala. From the turn of the century onward, an increasingly specialized form of natural science developed at an accelerating

Students at Physicum, c. 1910.

113

pace, and in several areas attracted international attention. Foreign students came to Uppsala as in the 18th century. Through German, French and later English, means of communication were provided that crossed all linguistic frontiers. Science could now quite literally reach out to the world at large.

ASTRONOMY AND METEOROLOGY

From the 1880s, astronomy entered a new and active period under Professor Nils Dunér. In addition to important investigations into solar rotation, Dunér made extensive studies of stellar spectra and developed the Uppsala Observatory into an international centre for stellar astronomy. Since about 1910, extragalactic research has played a dominant role. That there might exist other worlds beyond our own was an idea that had been launched at the close of the 16th century. The idea was once again rigorously debated at the beginning of the present century: might there be stellar systems outside our "own" Milky Way? Opinions were divided—it was indeed an entire world picture they were debating. By making pioneering measurements of distances and dimensions in the so-called Andromeda Galaxy, among others, the Uppsala researcher, Knut Lundmark, was regarded as having settled the question in the 1920s. There were unquestionably other stellar systems and perhaps even an infinite number of them.

Within the discipline of astronomy, a separate Chair of Meteorology was created in 1878 and a meteorological observatory built in the Observatory Park. Hugo Hildebrandsson was appointed professor, along with Dunér, the most notable natural scientist in Uppsala around the turn of the century. Hildebrandsson instituted a unique international collaboration

114

within meteorology in order to create a comprehensive picture of phenomena in the upper atmosphere. The "cloud year" of 1896–97, initiated by him, was epoch-making. Simultaneous measurements were made all over Europe, partly by means of air balloons released at various points. The classification of cloud formations elaborated by Hildebrandsson was adopted internationally in 1891. This constituted a pioneer work within photography; for the first time ever, the new art of photography was used in the service of research.

PHYSICS

Anders Jonas Ångström (cf. p. 89) helped physics in Sweden to take a huge leap forward. The number of students increased steeply from the 1880s and in the laboratories they had to jostle around the few work-benches. The situation was becoming catastrophic when in 1905 Parliament finally allotted the necessary fund for new buildings. Three years later Physicum was ready, and for the first time physics had its own departmental premises. Right from the start this building was praised for its practical design. It housed special rooms for spectral analysis and magnetic measurements, a duct passing right through the building for experiments in gravity, a special tower for observations of solar radiation, and much else.

The spectroscopic research initiated by Ångström has remained one of the main activities right up to the present day. The line passes in direct continuity from Anders Jonas to his son Knut Ångström, and further to Manne Siegbahn and then to his son Kai Siegbahn. By means of increasingly sophisticated instruments and methods (Roentgen spectroscopy, electron spectroscopy) it has become possible to investigate elements of

ever more complex structure, investigations that have been of great importance for the exploration of the structure of materials and which today have found application in nuclear physics. In 1924 Manne Siegbahn was awarded the Nobel Prize for Physics and his son Kai followed in 1981.

CHEMISTRY

In its new home, research in chemistry expanded confidently. In the 1860s, laboratory experiments for students were introduced; the influx was so great that it was found necessary to resort to laboratory periods during the Christmas holidays. The peak was reached in the mid-1880s, with over 100 newly registered students, an enormous increase in view of the situation at the Department only a few decades earlier. The importance of chemistry for industry became increasingly obvious and certainly favoured the Department which around 1900 again applied to Parliament for new and more modern premises. The new Chemicum, the Department's third chronologically, was inaugurated in 1904.

The man responsible for the expansion of chemistry as a discipline was Per Cleve, Professor of General Chemistry from 1874. Cleve carried out important investigations into the chemistry of earth metals and succeeded in isolating several new elements. It also fell to him to take on responsibility for the young Svante Arrhenius when in 1884 the latter wished to defend his thesis *Recherches sur la conductibilité galvanique des électrolytes*. This thesis contained the basic ideas of the so-called theory of electrolytic dissociation, which came to reshape elec-

Manne Siegbahn with his son Kai Siegbahn, 1960.

117

trochemistry and which also contained the solution to a number of basic problems in chemistry. But the import of the thesis was way above the heads of the professors and failed to qualify Arrhenius as an Associate Professor. He therefore sent his thesis to the world-famous chemist Wilhelm Ostwald in Riga, who immediately set off for Uppsala to expound Arrhenius' achievement for the ignorant. A few months later Arrhenius was awarded a personal Associate Professorship in Physical Chemistry. In 1903 he was awarded the Nobel Prize for Chemistry; by that time however, he had long been associated with Stockholm University.

PHYSICAL CHEMISTRY AND BIOCHEMISTRY— THE SVEDBERG AND ARNE TISELIUS

The development of physical chemistry initiated by Arrhenius was continued at the Uppsala Department of Chemistry by The Svedberg. Svedberg defended his thesis in 1907 after only three years at the University and in 1912 was awarded a personal professorship in Physical Chemistry. His unusual versatility was made use of a number of times in research assignments. Thus he elaborated a photographic technique that made it possible to produce a facsimile reproduction of Codex Argenteus (the Silver Bible). Another project which he led was to devise a method for the production of synthetic rubber during the import crisis occasioned by the Second World War. In the late 1940s Svedberg transferred his attention to nuclear research at the Gustaf Werner Institute for Nuclear Chemistry. In 1926 he was awarded the Nobel Prize for Chemistry.

Svedberg's main area of activity was within colloid chemistry, where in earlier work he had attempted to prove the con-

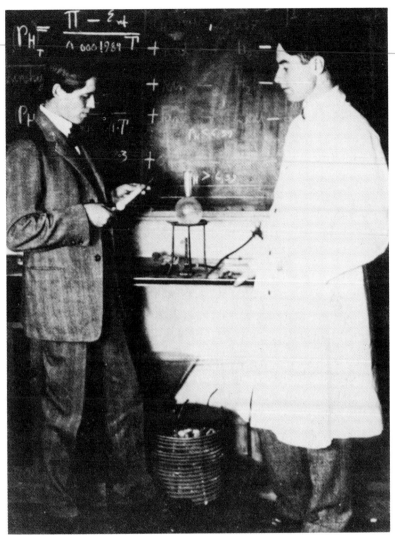

The Svedberg and Arne Tiselius in Svedberg's laboratory, 1926.

troversial molecular theory. About 1923 he devised a method whereby through ultracentrifugation the size and shape of molecules could be determined. Samples were enclosed in a capsule inside a steel rotor that was spun at exceptionally high speed. In the resulting centrifugal field, the molecules were hurled out toward the rotor's periphery where they could be measured by photography of the sediments. Ultracentrifugation has since been developed in stages and can reach rotation speeds corresponding to almost a millionfold of gravity. The method has been of great importance in modern biochemistry and molecular biology, among other applications.

Svedberg's laboratory (from 1932 the Department of Physical Chemistry) became one of the foremost centres in the world for research concerning high molecular elements and attracted large numbers of foreign researchers to Uppsala.

Svedberg's foremost successor was Arne Tiselius. He developed new techniques (electrophoresis, chromatography) for the separation and analysis of biochemically important substances, especially albuminous substances. The apparatus he constructed for electrophoresis has found far-reaching international application. It is constructed on the principle that the protein molecules move in an electrical field between two electrodes. Their movements are measured photographically, to give both qualitative and quantitive information about the various components. In this way Tiselius could demonstrate that human serum contains at least four protein components which he designated albumin, α-, β- and γ-globulin, and furthermore that the antibodies so formed in reaction to infection are γ-globulins. The method has opened up completely new avenues for the biological and medical investigation of proteins, including enzymes and virus proteins. Tiselius became in 1938 the first holder of a donative professorship in biochemistry. A Nobel

120

Prize in Chemistry followed in 1948. Since that time the development of biochemical separation techniques has been a key research area in Uppsala.

MEDICINE

As regards Medicine it soon became evident that in the building of the University Hospital (see p. 91), the resources made available had been insufficient. Among other things, the inadequate sanitary arrangements, combined with overcrowding even as early as in the 1880s, led to epidemics among the patients. After protracted negotiations with both County and State authorities, extensive building works were put in hand in the early 1890s, including maternity wards, and special departments for Paediatrics, Obstetrics and Ophthalmiatrics were set up. Parallel with the increasing numbers of patients, increasing specialization and the need for technically functional equipment, the hospital has had to wage a never-ceasing struggle to satisfy the demand by further building work and re-equipment.

The practical consequences of the advances made in the medical sphere were most evident in surgery. The introduction of antiseptics and effective methods of narcosis had a revolutionary effect on the prospects for surgical operations. Now it became possible to undertake more complicated interventions, for instance in the abdomen and brain. At the turn of the century, the Head of the Department was Karl Gustaf Lennander, responsible for important advances in abdominal surgery. In 1889 he successfully carried out the first appendectomy in Sweden. During the 1890s surgeons could put to good use yet another pioneering technique—Roentgen photography. In 1897 Lennander operated for the first time on a patient in

Medical students at the Academic Hospital, 1890, receive instruction in surgical operations from Professor Karl Gustaf Lennander.

whom the cause of the trouble, in this case a revolver bullet in the back of the head, had been localized by means of Roentgenography, or X-ray as it is more popularly known.

Ophthalmiatry, dealing with the healing of diseases of the eye, was the first special area detached from General Medicine. First incumbent of the professorial chair (1894) was Allvar Gullstrand. He worked at first with clinical ophthalmic medicine and surgery, but later transferred to purely theoretical research. It was Gullstrand who elaborated a theory for astigmatism and the diffraction of light in the eye (optical dioptrics), which formed the basis of the modern production of spectacles. He also constructed several important instruments, including a non-reflective ophthalmoscope which gave a sharp image of the fundus and made it possible to diagnose a number of eye diseases. In 1911 Gullstrand was awarded the Nobel Prize in Physiology and Medicine; in addition he achieved notoriety for his tenacious and forceful opposition to Einstein's theory of relativity, and by doing so contributed to the considerable delay in awarding the Nobel Prize to Einstein.

Other disciplines that became autonomous around the turn of the century were Paediatrics and Obstetrics. Paediatrics did much to reduce the still high mortality figures of the time. Obstetrics developed rapidly and in this connection the introduction of antiseptics was of the greatest importance, partly in eliminating the feared puerperal fever, but also for making caesarean sections possible. Other disciplines of great importance for public health and which were detached to form Departments were Bacteriology and Lung Medicine.

In public health and preventive medicine too, there was much progress. The application of the erythrocyte sedimentation phenomenon was to prove of great importance as a diagnostic tool. It had long been known that blood, when left in a vessel without coagulating, will gradually separate into layers. In the 1920's the pathologist Robin Fåhraeus commenced an intensive research programme to elucidate the conditions of blood separation. He established an analytical method based on the speed at which the red corpuscles settle, measured in mm/hour, and showed that deviations from the normal value of sedimentation are indicative of a morbid condition. The method soon spread throughout the world and nowadays is a routine component in all health checks.

Expansion and Reforms

After the Second World War

By Anders Lundgren

The changes undergone by Uppsala University since the Second World War are perhaps more momentous than any others in its long history. They can best be described as changes of an expansive nature.

The most spectacular feature of these developments has been the vast increase in the student population—from about 4,000 in 1945 to over 20,000 during the hectic years around 1970. Under the chancellorship of Professor Torgny Segerstedt, from 1955 to 1978, more undergraduates were admitted to the University than during the rectorial terms of all previous chancellors taken together, since 1477. With some justification therefore, one can apply the term explosion rather than expansion to this development.

Its chief causes were the sudden increase in the birth-rate during the 1940s and a series of primary and secondary education reforms which significantly broadened the range and number of students recruited to the University. Of importance also were a series of educational measures, above all in the form of scholarships and study loans. Nowadays the only expenses the undergraduate is obliged to meet are membership fees of his own representative organization, the Students' Union, and of

124

Rector Torgny Segerstedt speaking at the University's 500-Year-Jubilee 1977.

his own student "Nation" or club (whose membership is based broadly on geographical affiliation). Despite remedial measures, the social composition of the student population has not altered essentially, possibly because of antipathy among sections of the public at large toward advanced studies, an attitude that has not kept pace with social reforms and changes in the law.

The earlier academic organization was obviously not suited to cope with such a huge influx of undergraduates. Radical changes were necessary and a prominent feature of the University's postwar history has been the seemingly interminable changes in its organization and administration. Characteristic of these changes has been the increase in the number of disciplines, especially within the Faculties of Natural Sciences and of the Social Sciences. A number of educational reforms and new forms of university government have also been introduced.

During the first years after the Second World War, a continuous expansion of higher education and research took place. The state commission of inquiry that paved the way for the parliamentary bill of 1945 was entitled "The 1945 University Inquiry".

The reforms that followed during the late 1940s favoured the Arts and Sciences in particular, which were given several new professorial chairs, though Medicine, Theology and Law also received some new, higher posts. Of even greater importance, perhaps, were the preparations made for improved research appointments, partly by establishing a number of associate professorships (at the time called research scholarships), partly by awarding scholarships to those reading for a licentiate degree, and also for those with a Fil lic degree and working on their doctoral thesis, the so-called licentiate and doctoral scholarships.

126

By the mid-1950s it was felt that the time was ripe for a new commission of inquiry, and this was known as "the 1955 University Commission." The decisions reached by Parliament on the basis of the Commission's proposals, involved, first and foremost, educational improvements whose expressed intention was to improve teaching at the basic level.

One remarkable product of the Commission's initial work was the model for the calculation and apportioning of teaching posts in relation to the numbers of students, which was termed "university automation". Its consequence was that for the larger disciplines within the Faculties of Arts and Sciences, formulas were applied that laid down how many teachers were required for a given number of students. Furthermore, special teaching posts were created (senior lecturers) in those disciplines which had especially many students. All these measures were intended to help the students complete their studies within a reasonable period of time.

The 1955 Commission also proposed a number of other changes within the University's internal organization. As early as 1956 the Faculty of Arts and Sciences had been split into two faculties, one for Arts and one for Mathematics and the Natural Sciences. This meant the end of the old division into four faculties, which had been a tradition since the Middle Ages. Now the planners proceeded with their differentiating, detaching the Social Sciences and Behavioural Sciences from the Faculty of Arts and Sciences and forming a Faculty for the Social Sciences *per se* in 1964. A seventh faculty, for Pharmaceutics, was founded in 1968, by transferring the Pharmaceutical Department from Stockholm and incorporating it with Uppsala University.

The office of Chancellor which right up to the 1950s had been held by an elected representative of the University, the

University Chancellor, with his little staff of officials, was now transformed into a large, centrally organized civil service department, the University Chancellery, later renamed The National Board for Universities and Colleges, (*Universitets- och högskoleämbetet*, UHÄ). The Vice-Chancellor thus became a state-employed civil servant, with the status of a director-general, and appointed by the Government.

Even at the local level, organizational changes were pushed through. The Larger and Smaller Senates and the Finance Committee were replaced by a single Senate which became in effect the University's governing body. Its members were the Vice-Chancellor, Pro-Vice-Vice-Chancellor, deans of the faculties and sections, and the new head of administration. The latter post was created in 1964 at the Universities of Lund and Uppsala, with the title University Councillor. At both these seats of learning the University Councillor was also given a position as member of the Vice-Chancellery. The Vice-Chancellor still made his decisions in discharging his official duties— but in the presence of the administrative University Councillor. The post of Head of the Administration was created because it was considered necessary for the Vice-Chancellor to have someone to help him with his growing financial and administrative burdens.

Even the education of future researchers was reorganized. The special commission of inquiry set up in 1963 to investigate the prospects for and organization of research put forward its proposals in 1969. These abolished the old licentiate degree, replacing it with a new procedure by which the student was admitted directly to doctoral studies following his or her bachelor degree and after formal application to train as a research worker. The student would be expected subsequently to pass doctoral examinations, including a dissertation, after four years of studies. After that, the way would be open for a research career via appointments as research assistant. The value of these new arrangements and their actual value as a means to promote quality have often been questioned in recent years.

Following in the wake of the 1955 Commission of Inquiry came another, appointed in 1963, which presented its far-reaching proposals in 1968. This received the appellation UKAS (*Universitets-Kanslersämbetets Arbetsgrupp för fasta Studiegångar*, meaning roughly the Chancellor's Working Committee for Fixed Studies). The new proposals for University reform put forward by UKAS met determined opposition. They contained many novel and radical ideas, such as the establishment of fixed courses of education, adaptation of studies to suit the world of business and industry, and a certain degree of exclusion, which meant that student who failed to live up to expectations would be excluded from further studies.

It so happened that these proposals were presented at the same time as one of the most sensational ideological debates of postwar years was raging at the University—the so-called Student Revolt of 1968. Since the mid-1960s a vigorous and strongly critical student movement had developed, not only on the Continent, but also here in Uppsala. Its fundamental features were marxist, but its fires had been kindled chiefly by the war in Vietnam and events in Latin America. The University was seen to be an integral part of an unjust society that must be changed. It was an optimistic movement—all too optimistic as it proved—that made strong demands for political commitment and direct action. The protests against the UKAS proposals, which were regarded as buttressing an already unjust society, were on this account extremely powerful.

The lasting value of the 1968 revolt (of which the protests

129

against UKAS were only a part) is still a matter for lively debate even today, twenty years later. But it cannot be denied that the ideas and attitudes of that period, so impassioned and impatient, are a far cry from the even tenor of life of present-day students. One could perhaps wish for a little more of the sharpness of debate, the will to criticize and the passion of the 1968 movement in the students of today—even if the size and significance of the movement tended to be overestimated then, its goals set too high, and its methods often questionable.

But it would be wrong to dismiss the events of 1968 as expressions of youthful foolishness, or as a passing fad. What happened then led to increased debate and a questioning attitude towards traditional research, both as to content and method. At worst, the critics entered a cul-de-sac, but at their best they raised constructive criticisms which, in the long term, promoted research within the Arts and Sciences and Social Sciences, even though the effects were not of a kind to lead to a world revolution led by university students! Most of the active young researchers at Uppsala were influenced in various ways by these debates. In like manner, these activities of the students had an influence on one development which as it transpired was already in motion but which now accelerated, viz. the increased democratization of the decision-making process at the University.

To what extent opinion against UKAS was responsible for any of the changes effected in the proposals by the time they were presented in the form of PUKAS (the added initial referring to the then Minister of Education, Olof Palme), cannot be said with certainty, but it cannot be denied that PUKAS restored a little of the freedom of choice as regards studies that UKAS would have restricted. Moreover, both the students, via their representatives in the Students' Union, and the spokes-

130

men for the employees of the University procured both a seat and a voice in several decision-making bodies, from governing boards of the Departments to the Senate itself.

Nevertheless PUKAS had many faults. At a time of such rapid expansion it was difficult to find equally quickly a satisfactory organizational form. The 1968 Commisssion of Inquiry, already sitting, which commonly went under the title U68 (the 1968 Educational Commission), presented in 1973 a proposal that meant the gathering of all post-sixth form studies in Sweden under one head, in a unified high school organization of Higher Education, though divided into geographical regions, each led by a regional Board. It was proposed that the public interest should be accorded increased influence, that admission to the centres of higher education should be regulated, and that adaption to the needs of the professions should be further accentuated. Yet at the same time, larger sections of society should be given access to university studies—previous experience of employment (in other avenues of life) would be counted as a merit when applying for admission.

The students were not so strongly critical of this Commission as of its predecessor, but from the University as a whole, prolonged and stubborn opposition was offered. One of the more eminent opponents in Uppsala was its doughty Vice-Chancellor, Torgny Segerstedt. Critics of the proposals believed that the University would become far too dependent on the State. It was also felt that decentralization would mean a serious dilution of resources and consequently an overall lowering of standards within the Swedish university world.

The proponents of reform maintained that universities, by increasing their collaboration with the world around them and by allowing sections of the general public to have a voice in decision-making bodies, would gain in experience and this in

New departments: the Biomedical Centre (BMC) and the Centre of the Humanities and Social Sciences (HSC).

the long run would enrich university life—and thereby society at large.

The aforementioned reform was put into effect on July 1, 1977, just when Uppsala University was preoccupied with celebrating the 500th anniversary of its foundation. Allusion has sometimes been made to "growing pains" when characterizing the problems faced by the University during the decade starting in the mid-1950s. Most tangible of all perhaps were the sheer physical problems of premises and housing. The lack of residential accommodation for the students was a big problem for many a year, despite the sharp increase in newly built student rooms made available, partly by the individual student "Nations" (regional student clubs), and partly through the agency of the "Student Town Foundation".

The same overcrowded conditions obtained as regards classrooms, laboratories, offices for lecturers, libraries etc. In this area too, vigorous efforts were necessary. During the 1960s and 1970s especially, large-scale building operations were carried out to supply accommodation for the increasing numbers of students and to meet the needs of the dynamically expanding research work taking place in the seven faculties.

Considerable building was also carried out on behalf of the Natural Science faculties, to keep pace with the expanding research in that area. These works included, starting in the mid-1960s, the large Biomedical Centre. Teknikum, intended for the training of civil engineers, was ready in 1970; and more recently, during the 1980s, a large new particle accelerator has been built.

The expansion of the humanistic disciplines led to the establishment of the Centre for the Humanities and Social Sciences, (HSC), which was ready for use in 1976. More recently, a centre for Mathematics and Media Technology (MIC) has

133

been established in a renovated, former military garrison. In another part of the same area, close to the University Hospital and the Castle, is a newly created Science Park, named Glunten (after one of the two chief characters in a collection of student songs from the late 19th century). This centre is a result of the increasing cooperation between the University and society.

That society and research have to some extent differing needs is reflected in the history of Uppsala University. Society has always made—and still makes—legitimate demands on universities, which are entirely dependent on public support for their very existence. The University therefore has self-evident obligations vis-à-vis its employer, i.e. the State. The concept of a completely free and unfettered university is a myth. Nevertheless, it can rightly be maintained that it is the self-evident duty of the University to promote inquiry and an unbiassed investigation of reality with the object of influencing the development of society, and this too must also be respected. If it is not, then research can be exploited for electoral purposes or, even worse, become an uncritical megaphone for the present-day rulers of society. There is no lack of historical precedent.

It is true that society can survive without an active university, but it would be a society with considerable deficiencies. It is equally true that scientists and thinkers have by their own initiative succeeded in creating a university. The striving to achieve a balance between the demands of society and of scholarship has set its mark on the life of Uppsala University—and has done so over the centuries. The University has worked best when these two demands have coincided so as to enrich each other.

The students greeting Spring.